ENDORSEMENTS

The apostle Paul encouraged all Christians to "earnestly desire spiritual gifts, especially that you may prophesy" (1 Corinthians 14:1). It is obvious that we live in times of great change and great anxiety—prophetic times. Insight into the mind of God and an understanding of His ways is ever so needed today. That is why I am so glad Joan Hunter has chosen to release a guide for believers who want to learn how to minister prophetically.

You Can Prophesy will provide you with a solid foundation of practical and time-tested guidelines. It will encourage you to grow prophetically and at the same time help you avoid many of the pitfalls of prophetic ministry. Be bold in prayer, act in faith, and prophesy the word of God to others with all love. When you do, you will help change lives and create an atmosphere of glory for the kingdom to inhabit wherever you go!

JOSHUA MILLS
New Wine International
JoshuaMills.com

Joan Hunter has done it again and has written a masterpiece that will blow you socks off! She will take you step by step into fully understanding the prophetic in ways you never have before. Her no-nonsense direct approach will answer the questions you always wondered about but never had the answers to.

If you are ready for an adventure in the prophetic, this book is for you! I highly recommend this book to beginners and experts in the prophetic!

DR. DAVID HERZOG
Author of *Glory Invasion*
theGloryZone.org, Sedona, Arizona

A lot of prophetic people have written on prophecy and how to prophesy. But few have written in such an easy-to-understand style as Joan Hunter. In her classic storytelling way, Joan completely uncomplicates the subject of prophesying. In fact, her book title simply gives away her straight-forward style. The bottom line, Joan points out, is that *you can prophesy!*

Joan takes the reader through what could be a college course on prophesying, but with such easy-to-follow guidelines and principles that you've just got to have this book, both for yourself right now, for your reference library, and then another as a gift for a friend.

Joan teaches in this book that your words have power; the same creative power that flows from the mouth of God flows from you! It's time for you to start using the power that flows out of you from the Lord. After you've read this book, you'll be walking up to your friends and telling them, "You too can prophesy!"

STEVE SHULTZ
The Elijah List
ElijahList.com

YOU CAN Prophesy!

LEARNING TO SHARE GOD'S HEART TO CHANGE LIVES

JOAN HUNTER

WITH KELLEY MURRELL AND MELODY BARKER

YOU CAN *Prophesy*
LEARNING TO SHARE GOD'S HEART TO CHANGE LIVES

ISBN: 978-0-9963423-5-3

Copyright © 2016 by Joan Hunter

Published by Hunter Books
PO Box 411
Pinehurst, TX 77362 USA
www.joanhunter.org

Unless otherwise indicated, all Scripture is taken from THE HOLY BIBLE, NEW INTERNATIONAL VERSION®, NIV® Copyright © 1973, 1978, 1984, 2011 by Biblica, Inc.™ Used by permission. All rights reserved worldwide. Scripture quotations marked NKJV are from the New King James Version. Copyright © 1982 by Thomas Nelson, Inc. Used by permission. All rights reserved. Scripture quotations marked MSG are from THE MESSAGE. Copyright © by Eugene H. Peterson 1993, 1994, 1995, 1996, 2000, 2001, 2002. Used by permission of NavPress Publishing Group. Scripture marked KJV is taken from the King James Version of the Bible, which is in the public domain. Scripture quotations marked TLB are from The Living Bible copyright © 1971 by Tyndale House Foundation. Used by permission of Tyndale House Publishers Inc., Carol Stream, Illinois 60188. All rights reserved. Scripture quotations marked NLT are taken from the Holy Bible, New Living Translation, copyright © 1996, 2004, 2007 by Tyndale House Foundation. Used by permission of Tyndale House Publishers, Inc., Carol Stream, Illinois 60188, USA. All rights reserved. Scripture marked VOICE is from The Voice™. Copyright © 2008 by Ecclesia Bible Society. Used by permission. All rights reserved. Scripture marked NIRV is from the Holy Bible, NEW INTERNATIONAL READER'S VERSION®. Copyright © 1996, 1998 Biblica. All rights reserved throughout the world. Used by permission of Biblica. All marks of emphasis in the text (bold, italics, all caps) are the authors'.

Cover design by Yvonne Parks at www.pearcreative.ca
Interior design by Katherine Lloyed at www.theDESKonline.com

Printed in the United States of America

CONTENTS

ACKNOWLEDGMENTS

Very few books are written without the combined efforts and talents of a team of people (transcribers, editors, designers, publishers, etc.). I have been blessed to have written many books through the years. I have always found the process much easier with the help of an anointed team of men and women who work with me to see God's vision revealed through the written word. This book is no exception.

This has been a joint effort from day one. I want to acknowledge those who have contributed their time, knowledge, content, and revelation to this project. I give thanks and pray a special blessing over these men and women for sharing their knowledge, gifts, and abilities to see this project through to completion.

A special word of thanks to Dr. Krista Abbott and Naida Johnson for all their hard work on this manuscript.

FOREWORD BY PATRICIA KING

*O*ver forty years ago as a brand new Christian, I received some powerful and profound prophetic words declaring my potential destiny in Christ. These words were life-transforming to say the least! I carefully transcribed them in longhand from the audio recordings and to this day I have them filed and often review them. All of them have come to pass in part or in whole. It was not only the impact of the anointed words that affected me so deeply, but also the heavenly emotions that filled my heart and the tangible presence of God that was so very evident while I was receiving the inspired, prophetic words.

From those early years until now I have been in love with prophetic ministry! You can imagine how elated I was to discover soon into my walk with the Lord that "all can prophesy." I so wanted others to experience the glorious impact of blessed prophetic ministry like I had. As a result, I signed up for prophetic class at our church and learned how to prophesy. That's right, I "learned how." Many have the misconception that only specially chosen and anointed ministers can prophesy. They also mistakenly believe that you can only prophesy when a special unction from heaven comes upon you.

In our Bible classes we learned that you can activate the prophetic gift by faith and that *all* believers are able to prophesy.

Those evening classes were so enjoyable. The operation of the prophetic gift invites the Holy Spirit to invade gatherings with His love, presence, and power—and did we ever experience tall of those attributes regularly! Our entire church became acquainted with prophetic ministry and we enjoyed wonderful outpourings of the Spirit.

Years later, we were exhorted to take the prophetic to the streets—after all, our light belongs in the darkness. We prophesied to the lost, offering them encouragement as we pointed them to Jesus. While prophesying over their lives, they would be astounded at what they heard, felt, and experienced. Many of them came to know Jesus as their personal Savior. We prophesied the Word of the Lord on the streets, at parks and beaches, psychic fairs, tattoo parlors, new age book stores, brothels, and even at porn conventions. It was amazing to see those who were trapped in darkness come to know the Lord or at the least to be touched by Him. For many those moments were their first introduction to God.

The New Testament tells us that prophecies are to edify, exhort, and comfort, and that has certainly been my experience. Both the church and the world need to hear good news! They need to know how God thinks about them and what He has for their futures. They need hope … they need *Him*!

I am so glad *You Can Prophesy* by Joan Hunter, with Kelley Murrell and Melody Barker, is in your hand right now. If you desire to activate the prophetic and understand its purposes, this book is for you! May you become a blessing to many as you step out in faith and prophesy. YOU CAN!

PATRICIA KING
Author, motivational speaker, media host, and producer
PatriciaKing.com

FOREWORD BY JAMES W. GOLL

*T*oday we live in an unparalleled time where there is a global prophetic movement built upon previous moves of the Holy Spirit of church history. Wave upon wave of God's glorious presence combined with unfolding revelatory truths from the written Word of God help to create an atmosphere where all things are possible.

Many leaders consider 1988 as a demarcation in time where this modern-day phenomena had its birth in multiple locations and diverse ministries. I had the honor and privilege of being one of the pioneers in the wonder years of the "Kansas City prophets" when the world came to our doorstep to witness and partake of the seer dimension of the prophetic. Much has changed in the past thirty years. Back then we had a few highly gifted prophetic leaders on platforms and conference stages.

Today we have an entire generation in the worldwide body of Christ who has learned that they too can prophesy and declare the revelatory ways of the Holy Spirit. Today we have equippers who not only have "done the stuff," but now have the capacity and experience to teach and impart to others what they have learned by trial and error. It is a new day!

Paul the apostle stated you have many instructors but few fathers (see 1 Corinthians 4:15). The earlier charismatic

movement birthed in the 1960s was primarily a teaching movement with an emphasis on the baptism in the Holy Spirit along
with the empowering of the gifts of the Spirit. We had the great
blessing of having many teachers, but we had the deficit of not
having many true fathers and mothers.

The book of Genesis refers to our Lord Almighty as the God
of three generations in a generation: the God of Abraham, Isaac,
and Jacob. Yes, when we want to see a sustained move of the Holy
Spirit, it requires generational synergy or the joining of the generations. It is the biblical model and it works! In the charismatic
movement, for the most part, we had a few wonderfully graced
leaders who operated in the gifts of the Holy Spirit. Today, in this
generation, there is a huge difference. We have fathers and mothers of the faith who equip others to do what they have done and
continue to do! It is a time of multiplication.

The person who wrote this book was cut from this cloth. Joan
Hunter's mother and father were the infamous "Happy Hunters"
who not only walked in the gifts of the Spirit, but also turned
the corner to hosting large equipping gatherings. Joan Hunter, in
like manner, is an equipper in her generation, building upon the
platform of her parentage and of the previous moves of the Holy
Spirit. Ecclesiastes 4:9 declares, "Two are better than one." Why?
Because you bear forth more lasting fruit! Well, if that's true for
individuals, what about generations? When two and even three
generations are walking and working together, then we are moving in the power of the convergence of the ages!

In the past we had a few gifted leaders. Today we have an
emerging army of God (see Ezekiel 37) who understands that all
may prophesy (see 1 Corinthians 14:31). Joan beautifully paints a
glorious picture for us in this book where there exists a diversity
of prophetic anointings. We have prophetic evangelists, prophetic

faith, intimacy in the prophetic, and prophetic activation.

So devour this book, drink deeply of its timeless truths, and then move forward into a new period of time in church history! This is a time when every dedicated believer may be equipped by our good, good Father God, keeping our eyes on the finished work of the cross of Jesus, and empowered with the gifts of the Holy Spirit—especially that we might prophesy!

DR. JAMES W. GOLL
Founder of Encounters Network
and international best-selling author
EncountersNetwork.com

INTRODUCTION

At the writing of this book, I have been in ministry for over forty years. I co-pastored a church for eighteen years and traveled the world with my parents for a large portion of that time. I launched my own ministry fifteen years ago. During this time, I have heard many prophecies delivered and seen many fulfilled. I have also delivered prophetic words to individuals throughout my ministry and have learned key principles related to effective prophetic ministry. I tell you this so you will know that I have had experience in the prophetic movement. The material shared in this book reflects that experience.

In addition to what I personally have learned, I have called on some of my Joan Hunter Ministries team members to share their knowledge and experiences. As you read, you will find some of their messages, revelations, and testimonies referenced or credited directly while others are woven into the content.

As you read, I pray you will develop a solid foundation upon which to measure the prophetic words you receive as well as those you release. Prophecy is alive and active in the body of Christ today. God is speaking. How you choose to receive and respond to the words He gives you can literally determine the course of your life.

Your words have power. The same creative power that flows

from the mouth of God flows from you. He made you in His image. As a believer, God has given you the same authority that Jesus had when He ministered on the earth.

As we lay a simple foundation and reveal important keys regarding prophecy, prepare your heart to walk in the power of the prophetic word.

CHAPTER 1

Prophetic Foundations

efore a contractor can build a house, blueprints or floor plans are designed by an experienced architect to guide the workers through the building process.

Once a contractor has studied the blueprints, he gathers the necessary materials, supplies, and resources to begin building. The initial steps might seem overwhelming to most of us.

However, before any visible construction can begin, something else must be in place. What is necessary before a building can be safely erected? The foundation. If the foundation is shaky or unstable, the whole structure will be unstable and eventually may collapse.

The foundation of any structure either supports or undermines the overall quality of the building. In other words, a grade B foundation cannot support a grade A structure. It can only support a grade B structure or less. If you want a solid, stable structure, you must have a solid, stable foundation.

God, the Master architect, has given us His blueprints, His

plans for our lives, in His Word. How we study His blueprints and build upon them is part of our joy and responsibility as believers.

"It is the glory of God to conceal a matter; to search out a matter is the glory of kings" (Proverbs 25:2).

This Scripture excites me because it reminds me that God has hidden treasures for us in His Word. As we search them out, we share in the glory (or privilege) of kings.

Through the next several chapters, we will search out the hidden things in the Scriptures regarding prophecy. From these discoveries, you will develop a solid foundation to understand prophecy and learn to use it to empower your life and the lives of those around you.

WHAT IS PROPHECY?

Dictionaries define *prophecy* as a prediction or the foretelling of a future event. Some references imply that these predictions are given under divine inspiration or through some supernatural experience with a divine being (God, angels, etc.). Others compare prophecy to fortune-telling or other forms of divination, which are not from God.

The dictionary definition is not entirely accurate, nor is it entirely wrong. I believe this basic humanistic definition can create, if one is not careful, a sense of a super-spiritual, scary, or mysterious experience.

Oftentimes, people overcomplicate prophecy or limit it to the foretelling of some faraway future event. Although prophecy does include having foreknowledge about future events, it is not limited to that function.

Prophecy is not overly complicated or spooky. Its definition as written in Scripture is very simple. First Corinthians

14:3 states, "The one who prophesies speaks to people for their strengthening, encouraging and comfort."

Does prophecy involve foretelling future events? Yes, it does. It also includes speaking words that strengthen, encourage, and comfort those around you.

The Scripture goes on to say, "The one who prophesies edifies the church" (1 Corinthians 14:4). Edification is any word or action that instructs or improves those who hear it. In addition to future events, prophetic ministry includes encouraging, strengthening, comforting, and edifying words spoken to you and through you for the benefit of others. A prophecy is meant for the benefit (or edification) of anyone who hears it.

I can vividly remember the first time I prophesied to another person when I suddenly realized the prophecy was for me also.

If you understand the definition of prophecy, you will realize how easy it is for anyone to prophesy. You do not have to be operating in the office of a prophet in order to operate in the gift of prophecy. All believers have the ability to decree the Word of God over atmospheres around them, but not all are functioning in the gift of prophecy or the office of a prophet.

SCRIPTURAL PROPHECIES

The Bible is full of prophecy. I encourage you to search out the prophecies and when fulfillment of each was manifested. It is a fascinating study and will open up many new facets of God's Word to your heart.

Many Old Testament prophecies about Jesus and His life were given hundreds of years before He set foot on planet earth. God's people waited and waited and waited. However, the prophets' words did come to pass.

Some prophets were considered crazy in their day. Jonah was swallowed by a whale. One went about in sackcloth and ashes. One ate locusts. Some dreamed dreams and others interpreted dreams. All of these revelations are messages God wanted us to know about.

Continue your research by studying the prophets of the church over the years. Some were fiery, others were quiet, but prophets have been present throughout church history. Discovering who they were, what they spoke, and how God fulfilled their messages will feed your faith and encourage you to be open to His voice.

OFFICE OF THE PROPHET VERSUS GIFT OF PROPHECY

Oftentimes people confuse the gift of prophecy or the ability to prophesy with being a "prophet." Some individuals have been gifted and called to operate in the office of a prophet. Other individuals operate or flow in the gift of prophecy but are not called to the office of a prophet. While you should desire to prophesy and have the ability to operate in that gift, you may not be called to walk in the office of prophet.

It is easy to identify the prophets who operated during biblical times. Most of them had books written by them, for them, or about them. It is not always easy to identify someone in modern times who is walking in that office. However, a few stand out as modern-day prophets. Their prophetic voice is not just a gift of prophecy. They are called to stand in the office of prophet and make declarations over cities, states, and nations of the world. They are held to a higher level of responsibility and accountability than others are. I honor and bless them as key prophetic voices for this generation.

So what distinguishes the two? How do we know when someone is operating in the gift of prophecy or is called to the office of prophet?

First, look at the gifts God has given to the church and how the gift of prophecy looks for the church. First Corinthians 12:7–11 (NKJV) reads:

> The manifestation of the Spirit is given to each one for the profit of all: for to one is given the word of wisdom through the Spirit, to another the word of knowledge through the same Spirit, to another faith by the same Spirit, to another gifts of healings by the same Spirit, to another the working of miracles, *to another prophecy*, to another discerning of spirits, to another different kinds of tongues, to another the interpretation of tongues. But one and the same Spirit works all these things, distributing to each one individually as He wills.

God gave many gifts to the church as well as to each person. After a gift is received, each person is responsible for operating in and developing that gift to maturity so God can use him or her freely and effectively in the kingdom of God.

People with the gift of prophecy will provide a "common good" service to the body of Christ. They will be closely tuned in to the Holy Spirit and be able to flow with God's heart for the person, circumstance, or situation requiring ministry at that specific time.

For example, I teach on various subjects. Moments before or sometimes during a message, the Holy Spirit will take me a different direction than what I prepared. Flowing with the Holy Spirit and being sensitive to what He is speaking at the time is important. The message that comes forth may be for one particular person in that service who needs to hear that word at that time. On other occasions, it may be a collective word for several people attending the meeting or for the church where I am ministering.

God is always speaking. As we listen and operate with sensitivity to His Spirit, He can speak through us. When we allow Him to speak through us, we are functioning in the gift of prophecy.

Some may confuse prophecy with a word of wisdom or a word of knowledge. Their meanings are similar yet different. A word of wisdom or a word of knowledge can be about something that happened in the past. Quite often, they reveal a situation needing prayer. For instance, I may know that someone in the audience has a back problem from a car accident; however, I do not know that person's identity. The individual with the problem has to accept the word, confirm it, and identify himself as the person needing prayer. I will then request that he come for ministry from me or one of the team members. Basically, facts about a person are discerned spiritually and shared with the group of people present. Often, more than one person can and will identify with the word given and want ministry.

Next we will consider the office of a prophet. What distinguishes a prophet from one who operates in the gift of prophecy?

There are five God-appointed "offices" of ministry noted in Ephesians 4:11–13 (NKJV):

He Himself gave some to be apostles, some prophets, some evangelists, and some pastors and teachers, for the equipping of the saints for the work of ministry, for the edifying of the body of Christ, till we all come to the unity of the faith and of the knowledge of the Son of

God, to a perfect man, to the measure of the stature of the fullness of Christ.

A prophet is one who speaks and decrees God's messages to His people, to the church, nations, and governments. It is important for those called to the office of prophet to guard the words they speak and be sure that the messages they convey are from the heart and will of God. The power of creation rests in the tongue of a prophet. When they speak, things happen and realities are manifested.

The anointing on the person called to the office of prophet is different from the gift of prophecy. When the one standing in the office of prophet speaks, his word becomes as described in Isaiah 55:11. "So is my word that goes out from my mouth: it will not return to me empty, but will accomplish what I desire and achieve the purpose for which I sent it."

Discernment and clear understanding of these roles are necessary in order to release the power of the prophetic in your life. You may be saying, "But Joan, I'm not a prophet and I don't think I have that gift." That does not mean that you cannot prophesy and decree/declare things over your life. You can, you will, and you probably already have without even realizing it!

In the chapters ahead, I will show you how your life can be empowered supernaturally through your decrees and declarations over yourself, the people you touch, and your environment. We will begin by discussing why every person should desire to prophesy.

CHAPTER 2

Understanding Prophecy

Why should you prophesy? How can it affect your life? Why is it important? If you do not realize how important it is, and understand how or why to use it, prophecy will not be a benefit for you. It is like having a tool with no idea how to use it or trying to put something together without the instructions. It will not work.

The Word of God says in 1 Corinthians 14:39, "Therefore, my brothers and sisters, be eager to prophesy." This means a believer should want to prophesy with a strong yearning or great desire.

Have you ever wanted something so much you could not think of anything else? When you desire something strongly, it can seem like an obsession. Most obsessions are not healthy, but we are talking about the good kind of preoccupation or focus that leads to life. This kind of passion pushes, drives, and motivates you to action. When you desire to prophesy or to obtain His gifts with fervency and passion, God will meet you at your point of desire and fulfill His promises as you seek Him with all your heart.

This kind of pursuit does not come without opposition. Do not lose focus. Remain fixed on what God has directed you to do. While writing this book, we have encountered many obstacles and roadblocks along the path to its completion. The pursuit of anything of lasting value generally requires great effort and perseverance in the face of unexpected obstacles.

Because we are training you and imparting knowledge to you, we face opposition. Knowledge is power. As you learn about prophecy, you discover God can speak through you. You can also use it to understand difficult situations and respond wisely, effectively, and efficiently. You can become very powerful in the kingdom of God and in your own life when you learn how to prophesy. As you develop a full understanding of prophecy and the value it gives a believer, you will be empowered at a level that threatens the enemy's plans. Prophecy will become another weapon in your armory to prepare you for battle.

GETTING STARTED

How do you begin? How do you decree and declare in a way that will transform your life? In what ways can you prophesy?

The starting point for all prophecy is speaking the Word of God over yourself and making it live within you. Find Scriptures in God's Word that speak to your situation. Take those Scriptures, personalize them, and speak them aloud every day over your life. Stand on His Word for the desired breakthrough or transformation in your life.

For example, if you believe God for healing in your life, find Scriptures on healing and speak them over yourself every day until you receive your healing. If you believe God fo breakthrough, find Scriptures on finances. Personalize them and speak them over yourself until you receive your financial breakthrough.

You personalize a Scripture by replacing words in the verse to speak directly to yourself. You can do this by replacing the word you with me or placing your name within the verse.

For example, Psalm 103:1–5 reads, "Praise the Lord, my soul; all my inmost being, praise his holy name. Praise the Lord, my soul, and forget not all his benefits—who forgives all your sins and heals all your diseases, who redeems your life from the pit and crowns you with love and compassion, who satisfies your desires with good things so that your youth is renewed like the eagle's."

If I were to personalize that passage, it would read like this: "Praise the Lord, soul; all my inmost being, praise his holy name. Praise the Lord, soul, and forget not all his benefits—who forgives all my sins and heals all my diseases, who redeems my life from the pit and crowns me with love and compassion, who satisfies my desires with good things so that my youth is renewed like the eagle's."

The changes are subtle but powerful. When your ears hear your voice speaking the Word of God directly to your life, something powerful happens in you and in your atmosphere.

To get started, think about the areas of your life you want transformed. Find Scriptures to stand on, write them out as personalized declarations, and speak them over yourself regularly. Look in the mirror and speak to the person looking back at you.

When you do this, you will see manifestations of what you are seeking, because there is power in your confession of the Word. Proverbs 18:21 (MSG) says, "Words kill, words give life;

they're either poison or fruit—you choose." Stop speaking death over your life, your finances, your health, your situations and circumstances. Instead, speak life! Encourage yourself in the Lord.

Prophecy can also be God giving you a specific word for the edification and encouragement of an individual or a group of people. If you are sensitive to the Holy Spirit and willing to help someone else, you can become a mouthpiece for Him to speak hope and encouragement to those around you.

The world has many hurting people. You encounter individuals every day in your job, while running errands, at church and school events, family functions—wherever you interact with people. Usually you will never know the devastation, challenges, or pain a person is dealing with on the inside. God wants you to deliver a perfect word to them through you. Be sensitive to His voice.

Leviticus 26:4 (KJV) says, "Then I will give you rain in due season, and the land shall yield her increase, and the trees of the field shall yield their fruit."

Plants need rain to grow and produce and sometimes simply survive the scorching heat of summer. Being yielded to the Holy Spirit and desiring to prophesy is important. You never know when the prophetic word of God's encouragement spoken through you will be the "rain" someone needs to make it through a difficult season or the gentle nudge needed to produce fruit in his or her life. Desire to prophesy. It is one of the greatest gifts you can give—not only to yourself, but also to others.

Prophecy is usually spontaneous, always divinely inspired, and given by the Holy Spirit from God's heart for a specific sit-uati It always has a purpose. It is not random. If God says ing to you, He wants you to do something. The only ques- need to ask are: What should I do? When should I act?

The book of Jonah gives an example of prophecy with a specific purpose. God told Jonah to go to Nineveh and "cry out against it" (1:2). God wanted Jonah to tell them of pending destruction because of their sin and rebellion. Jonah tried to ignore God and fled the other direction. He did not want to deliver such a message. However, God would not let him avoid his assignment. Jonah ended up in the belly of a whale until he finally submitted to God's plans. Once Jonah delivered God's message to Nineveh, the people repented and God spared them from destruction.

Jonah was God's mouthpiece, and delivering this prophetic word to the people of Nineveh had a specific purpose. It was not up to Jonah to make a decision. He wasn't there to wreak destruction or grant mercy to the people of Nineveh. In fact, Jonah got mad when God did not destroy Nineveh. God had chosen to forgive a nation that was an enemy of the Hebrews. When the prophecy did not manifest, Jonah appeared to be a false prophet and was probably embarrassed. God had to teach Jonah another hard lesson. He had to learn that God's love for people far outweighs His judgments. The ultimate outcome demonstrated God's heart of mercy and loving kindness.

When you deliver a prophetic word, you are just the mouthpiece. It is not up to you to bring it about or to determine the fate of the person who receives the message. The outcome of a prophetic word is dependent on God and the response of the person receiving the word. Although God selected you to be the mouthpiece for a purpose that you may or may not understand, He will ensure that the word is delivered. Do not be like Jonah and resist to the point of finding yourself in a precarious situation before accepting the mission. Maintain an open and willing heart to be a vessel for God to flow through and use.

WHEN GOD IS SPEAKING TO YOU

People frequently ask, "How do I know when God is speaking to me?" or "How can I know for sure that it is God telling me to do something?" God speaks to everyone in a way they will understand. He uniquely designed each of us and we all have different life experiences, circumstances, education, and cultural training. He is not going to communicate to me the same way He does to you. He will not speak to you the same way He speaks to your spouse or your children. But He will speak to you.

John 10:27 (TLB) says, "My sheep recognize my voice, and I know them, and they follow me." As you spend time with God, through reading His word, worship, prayer, or communing with Him in nature, you will develop a love language with Him that will leave no doubt when He is speaking to you. Communication with Him becomes natural over time. As you develop an intimate relationship with Him, you will recognize His leading in your life.

As a parent, you know the voices and the cries of your children because you have developed a close relationship with them. Married individuals know the voice of their spouses because they have developed a level of intimacy. They recognize each other's voices even in a crowded room.

Those same principles and concepts apply to your relationship with God. When you spend time with Him, you learn to distinguish His voice from all others. As your heart connects with His heart, you respond to the gentle whisper of His voice.

God can speak to you in many ways. He may give you a dream, flash a picture in front of you, or give you a Scripture. He may show you a sign that has special meaning to you or illuminate a truth to you when you see something in the natural. I call this a revelation. He may choose to speak directly to you in an audible voice or strongly impress something upon your heart. Receiving a word from another person (a stranger or a friend) is also common. A generic message on Facebook or in an e-mail can give you a special word for someone or for yourself. God can communicate to you in many ways, and He will use every means possible to get His message across to you.

If you are going to prophesy, it is important to recognize the voice of God as He speaks to you. Some people have told me they have a hard time hearing God's voice. In most cases, they are not taking the time or creating the space to listen to what God is saying to them. Or when God does speak to them, they do not obey His instructions. Disobedience shuts God out of anyone's life.

When a member of our ministry team hears a comment like that, they are likely to say, "Stop saying that! You are prophesying over yourself that you cannot hear God. You are saying with all the authority of Jesus Christ that you cannot hear Him. That is a word curse. This will continue to be a problem for you unless you change your confession."

Also, if you are busy talking, it is impossible to listen or hear God's voice. If you give somebody instructions and they keep talking over you, eventually you will say, "Go ahead and finish talking. When you want help and direction on this, I will give it to you. I will not talk over you."

If you are having a hard time hearing God, practice. Practice talking *with* Him, not just *to* Him. When you talk with someone, you speak and then listen for his or her response. As you practice listening and obeying, you will distinguish and hear God's voice. You may need to minimize distractions by changing your environment. Find a quiet place with no people, cell phones, televisions, or computers to distract you. Simply wait on God.

If you are waiting to hear the voice of God, you must listen more than talk. He is a gentleman and quietly waits to be heard. If you hear His voice and listen patiently to what He is saying, there is no reason for Him to talk over you. The Holy Spirit will speak to you in a still, small voice, rather than a loud, booming thunder that would probably scare you.

Elijah's story vividly demonstrates this principle. In I Kings 19, Elijah escaped from Jezebel when she wanted to kill all of God's prophets. Elijah was hiding, depressed and feeling all alone. God came to comfort him, but notice how God spoke to him.

> The Lord said, "Go out. Stand on the mountain in front of me. I am going to pass by." As the Lord approached, a very powerful wind tore the mountains apart. It broke up the rocks. But the Lord wasn't in the wind. After the wind there was an earthquake. But the Lord wasn't in the earthquake. After the earthquake a fire came. But the Lord wasn't in the fire. And after the fire there was only a gentle whisper. (1 Kings 19:11–12 NIRV)

Jesus taught that the kingdom of heaven is within us.

When He was asked by the Pharisees when the kingdom of God would come, He answered them and said, "The kingdom of God does not come with observation; nor will they say, 'See here!' or 'See there!' For indeed, the kingdom of God is within you." (Luke 17:20–21 NKJV).

You have to take a journey into your own heart to hear what God is saying to you. This requires shutting out the outside world for a few minutes or hours in order to connect with your heart. If you are born again and filled with the Spirit of God, your heart will guide you to His truth within you.

There must be focused times of listening for His word to come to you. This practice will prepare you for recognizing God's voice when He speaks to you in the midst of your daily activities. I enjoy those moments when I am simply going about His business and He suddenly drops something in front of me that illuminates a truth and provides insight, revelation, or new awareness. This new understanding may provide confirmation that I am headed in the right direction or correction if I am not. These are clear signs that God is speaking to me and working in my life.

When you receive a word from God, you may experience a shift physically, emotionally, or mentally. The sensation differs from person to person and can sometimes depend on the type of word God is about to deliver to you.

A physiological response in your body may alert you. Some people feel a wind blow over them while others feel warmth like a fire in their belly, mouth, or hands. Others may feel butterflies or get sweaty palms. These are all physical manifestations to alert you and confirm to you that the Holy Spirit is inspiring you to deliver a word. It can be a sign of confirmation that He desires to speak through you. I like to think of it as His subtle way of saying, "I am encouraging you to do this. Speak now."

When you are surprised or scared, your body responds with a "fight or flight" reaction and an adrenaline rush. Either you will fight back or you will run. In this case, it is the Holy Spirit saying, "Get ready to run with this. I want you to take this message and do something with it." It is important to hear from Him, know He has a specific purpose, and then follow through to fulfill that purpose. Act quickly when God prompts you.

Sometimes He may give you a word that is for the future. When this is the case, you will sense a "hold on" or a "caution light" feeling in your spirit. In these cases, hold the message until He gives you the full release to share it. Some words are for a certain time, and if they are released too soon, they may not produce the result or the impact God intends. Be ready to speak a word when you receive it, but also be sensitive to hold fast when He encourages you to wait until an appointed time.

Always keep in mind that God speaks to you in a still small voice, a gentle whisper you hear deep in your heart. As you receive the word He is speaking to you, repeat that word to yourself, decree it into the atmosphere, and speak it over your life. When you follow these steps, you are actively engaging in the prophetic.

Another definition of prophecy is this: God speaks to you and you repeat what you have heard as He directs you.

CHAPTER 3

Purpose of Prophecy

*G*od speaks in many ways and for many purposes. Prophecy serves to encourage, edify, exhort, correct, and comfort. Prophecy can be a warning of things to come in the future and allows you an opportunity to make preparation or change. It can confirm decisions or actions when you are seeking God for direction. It is a message from God to you: a specific word to a specific person, or group of people, for a specific purpose. It is not "spooky spiritual," nor should it create fear. It is simply God's way to communicate things that are and things that will be. When you grasp this key concept, it becomes easier to flow with the Spirit of God as He speaks to you.

As you progress through this teaching, you will experience God and prophecy on a new level and in a new way. God will test your faith and your character with the word He gives you. You may be required to take a leap of faith to release the word He gives you, because it may not make sense to you. However, when released at the right time to the intended person, the word will make perfect sense to him or her.

A few weeks ago, someone shared a story with me. He had received a one-word prophecy for another individual. The word was *lemon*. As he received it and felt prompted to release it, he inquired of the Lord and asked for more information. When God gave no more information, he argued a bit with Him. God pushed him to deliver the single word to the intended person. Hesitantly, he walked up to the person and said something along the lines of "I am not sure what this means or why God wants me to tell you this, but God is telling me to say 'Lemon' to you." Both were surprised. But the person got excited and proceeded to explain.

That word was the exact answer this person had been seeking. He had been praying about buying a particular vehicle. He did not feel a full release to move forward with the purchase. When he heard the word *lemon*, he immediately realized God was warning him that the car was a lemon (informal definition for defective; not a good choice). By submitting in faith to God's leading, the person giving the prophecy discovered this one simple word was an answer to someone's prayers.

A single word can be a powerful prophetic answer to prayer. A couple was contemplating a serious move and sought God's guidance. They prayed for a sign from God and were attempting to wait patiently for His answer. They attended a meeting. One of the team members looked at them and reluctantly said, "Pineapple." The couple got excited and were nearly in tears. It took a while before they could give a coherent explanation. Their intended destination was Hawaii. The only place pineapples flourish is Hawaii! Up front, saying "pineapple" sounded silly. But one word of confirmation made an important change in their future.

WHO IS PROPHECY FOR?

Questions I am often asked include "Can anyone prophecy?" and "Is prophecy for everyone?" Most Christian circles believe prophecy can only flow through those who have a special calling on their lives or those who occupy the office of a prophet. Prophecy is not difficult or reserved for the elite or God's favorites. Prophesying is the spiritual inheritance of all believers!

First Corinthians 14:22 (NKJV) tells us, "Prophesying is not for unbelievers but for those who believe." In fact, the apostle Paul tells us to desire to prophesy. "Follow the way of love. You should also want the gifts the Holy Spirit gives. Most of all, you should want the gift of prophecy" (1 Corinthians 14:1 NIRV). Don't we want all the gifts He has for us? Prophecy is a gift from Him.

If Scripture instructs believers to desire to prophesy, it is obvious that the ability to prophesy is for everyone, not just a select few. Most people do not know how to prophesy or how to develop a prophetic ministry.

One purpose of this book is to help you learn how to prophesy over your day, your body, and your life. If you have not fully received your healing yet, continue to say, "Father, I thank You that today is the day of my healing. Today, every sign and symptom of this sickness will be gone, in Jesus' name." When you speak those words over your body, expect to see changes happen. Repeat those healing Scriptures, which are a prophecy to you from His Word.

WHY PROPHESY?

First Corinthians 14:3 tells us why we are called to prophesy. "The one who prophesies speaks to people for their strengthening, encouraging and comfort." Or, as the New King James

Version says, for "edification and exhortation and comfort." If you have been given a word but you aren't sure whether God has given it, ask yourself the following questions:

1. Is it edifying?

2. Does it exhort or correct in love?

3. Is it going to bring comfort to the person receiving it?

If you answer yes to each question, be assured the word is from God and He will give you the words to say and the appropriate moment in which to share them. There is no need to get nervous or upset about the experience.

"The Lord gives strength to his people; the Lord blesses his people with peace" (Psalm 29:11).

Prophetic ministry is also meant to bring peace or speak peace over difficult circumstances. In walking out the purpose and plan of God for your life, you will face challenging situations. These opportunities will increase your faith and allow you to exercise and develop the prophetic gift God has placed within you. As you speak to the circumstance and declare God's word over your environment, you are able to experience peace in the midst of the storm and reach a peaceful harbor.

"The peace of God, which transcends all understanding, will guard your hearts and your minds in Christ Jesus" (Philippians 4:7).

A few years ago, my daughter Melody realized the power of this verse as she trusted God during a trying time. She was standing in faith with her older sister, Charity, who was experiencing a difficult pregnancy with complications.

When Charity was pregnant with Presley, the doctor noticed she had spots on her brain. He explained, "Most babies grow out of this. If she doesn't, you can work with it and she can progress through these issues." As you can imagine, this was a devastating report for my daughter and son-in-law.

Their natural human response could have caused all sorts of negative thoughts about the possibilities and scenarios, which could affect their unborn baby. This precious child could have brain damage, disabilities, or other mental/physical limitations that could prevent normal growth or inhibit a healthy life.

As if that was not scary enough, the doctor also explained that the blood flow to and from the uterus through the umbilical cord was not functioning properly. The normal umbilical cord has one blood vessel carrying blood rich in oxygen and nutrients to the baby from the mother and two other pathways that carry deoxygenated blood and waste products from the baby back into the placenta. Unfortunately, one of the pathways was missing. There was only one channel in and one out.

As the doctors explained that the umbilical cord was not functioning as it should and the spots on Presley's brain were worrisome, my daughter's thoughts were going a hundred miles per hour with all the "what ifs" in this situation. Even in the midst of this bad news, my daughter was comforted because she knew the Scripture and found the peace of God that surpasses all understanding.

Rather than letting the doctor's words take root in her heart and mind and then proceed from her mouth, creating a "prophetic word" over their unborn child, she chose to grab hold of the truth in God's Word. She began to speak it forth, declaring (prophesying) health over Presley. The named Presley means "a place of peace, a peaceful pasture." It was as if the meaning of the baby's name was the prophetic word of assurance that everything was going to be all right. God was already prophesying through them to encourage them through the pregnancy.

God was telling her, "I am going to bring you to a place of peace, a peaceful pasture." Whenever my daughter talked, she spoke in faith. "God's peace surpasses all understanding, no matter what the doctors are saying. No matter what the facts are, His peace far exceeds all of our understanding."

You can guess what happened. The baby was born a happy, healthy, and well-adjusted child. Hallelujah! This illustrates the power of prophesying the Word of God over your situation and allowing the peace of God to reign over your circumstances.

Influencing Your Circumstance

It doesn't matter what your circumstances are. Or what the doctor's report says. Or what your accountant or lawyer says. No matter what your friends and family say, no matter what circumstance or trial you are facing, God's Word is your final authority. When you decree or declare (prophesy) His Word over your situation, you can walk in perfect peace, knowing that His love will overcome. His perfect plan will prevail in your life.

Keep speaking and declaring God's word over you, knowing these things are true. You are healed, you are free, you are blessed, and you are joyful! You are not what others say you are. You are whatever God's Word says you are. You become whatever you declare, decree, and prophesy over yourself.

I have prayed Philippians 4:7 over many people who have dealt with painful issues, or been unsure of what God called them to do, or were having family disputes. I told them, "This is a verse you need to own. It is the key to experiencing God's peace and knowing that He will see you through no matter what your current circumstances."

You can find the peace that God has for you by repeat.
aloud, right now:

God, I thank You that despite all of my circumstances and everything that I know in the natural, You are bringing Your peace beyond understanding into my life and resolving this situation according to Your Word.

CHAPTER 4

Your Role with the Prophetic Word

Prophetic ministry is an important component of the Christian life. But it is not meant to supersede Scripture as you seek the will of God for your life. Prophecy will always complement or confirm Scripture. It can also complement or confirm something God has already spoken to you about the path He wants you to follow. Prophecy does not replace God's written Word or what He has already placed within your heart.

Unfortunately, I have seen many Christians in search of "a word for their life" run from ministry to ministry or prophet to prophet hoping to get "a word" that will change their lives. God has already given us the Word in Jesus Christ. He is the only life-changing Word you really need. Everything else is extra, like gravy on your mashed potatoes.

I am not minimizing the importance of prophetic words. Instead, I want to encourage balance in dealing with prophetic ministry. The Holy Spirit in you will use you prophetically as long as you are willing to be sensitive and yield to His voice. In addition, take prophetic words you receive seriously. Write them down, meditate on them, pray over them, and decree them in the Spirit. In doing this, remember that all prophetic words should be considered *with* the Word of God, not apart from it.

BALANCING PROPHETIC WORDS WITH SCRIPTURE

As you receive prophetic words for your life and for the lives of those God places in your path, measure every word by Scripture. Here are a couple of important points to remember:

1. Prophecy is not equal to Scripture in its authority, power, or purpose.

2. Prophecy does not replace Scripture.

The Word of God must be maintained in its proper position, power, purpose, and authority for your life. His Word must be held in higher esteem than any other priority or directive in your life. Never elevate a prophetic word from man over the divinely inspired Word of God. The prophetic should complement the Word. If someone gives you a "prophetic word" that is contrary to Scripture, do not receive it in your spirit. Instead, use God's gift of discernment, put it aside, commit your ways to the Lord, and let Him direct your path.

What Happens When a Prophetic Word Is Unfulfilled?

A friend received some awesome prophetic words. When I heard them, I said, "This is such a good word, I want it to be mine." One word she received was for a call to greatness. I sat there thinking, *That's an awesome word! Me too, Lord!*

Yet difficult situations occurred in my friend's life, and none of those prophetic words were fulfilled. The failure was not because of anything she did. Uncontrollable circumstances removed key people from her life. This does not mean those prophetic words were wrong. It just meant that God would have to fulfill them in a different way.

God's word is His word. It may not always happen the way you think it should, but it will always come about if you respond correctly. God is a good God and He wants the best for His children. When you receive a word, do not concern yourself with how or when it will manifest, just trust that it will. God loves you and He will fulfill His word to you as long as you walk in faith and obedience.

A prophetic word given by someone else is not intended to be a spiritual compass for you. It should serve, rather, as confirmation of something God has already placed in your heart. Prophetic words are awesome, but it is not wise for you to use somebody else's compass to guide you or chart the direction of your life. Your responsibility as a believer is to receive the prophetic word for what it is. Always pray and confirm it with Scripture.

Receive the word, find a Scripture or Scriptures to support what it is saying, and take it to God, saying, "God, I know the plans and purpose that You have for me according to Scripture. I will not change my life because of other people's prophetic words for me. Instead, I choose to rely on Your Holy Spirit to lead me and cause this prophetic word to happen in Your perfect timing and in Your way."

God's Word stands forever and remains unchanged, so look at what Scripture says about your life prophetically. Understand that God's Word will be closer to your heart and more influential over your life than what any other person says or does.

Some people who have received prophetic words will say, "It did not happen. That word was never fulfilled." There are several things that can impact or affect a prophetic word and its fulfillment.

1. Inaction

Prophetic words sometimes require action from key people in your life. If those key people move on or do not cooperate with the plan of God, their choices do not nullify the word of God over your life, nor does it mean that the prophetic word will not be fulfilled. However, it may mean that there has to be an adjustment in the way it manifests in your life. God is faithful and will fulfill His promises.

2. Dishonoring the Prophet

Your treatment of a prophet will affect whether your prophecy will be fulfilled.

What do I mean? Let's examine an example. You receive a great word during a service. As you leave, you turn to your friend and start criticizing the prophet. "Did you see her hair? And those tattoos? Those clothes certainly weren't appropriate for such a meeting. I think she was chewing gum too! I don't believe a woman should be in such a position of leadership."

Oh, yes, people will make negative comments instead of praising God for a special word spoken through the prophet. Those critical comments can cut off any positive word God gave them.

You must honor and respect the prophet.

"Whoever welcomes a prophet as a prophet will receive a prophet's reward, and whoever welcomes a righteous person as a righteous person will receive a righteous person's reward" (Matthew 10:41).

"Do not touch My anointed ones, and do My prophets no harm" (1 Chronicles 16:22 NKJV).

The anointing on prophets or preachers or teachers flows from them to the listener, you, when you honor them and receive what they say to you. When you support them and help them fulfill God's call on their lives, part of their blessing flows through to you. This is a powerful truth in God's Word.

Once you have discerned that God has spoken through a prophet, receive that word as a special gift from God. Don't reject God by rejecting the person He sent to talk to you. Don't make fun of His representative. Would you criticize God? Would you make fun of God? If you do, you are welcoming His wrath. It is bad enough to unknowingly ignore His wooings and direction. But please don't mistreat another person. What you give, you will get.

3. Timing

The fulfillment of a prophetic word will usually not be on our timeline or schedule. The timing of a prophetic word and the manifestation of it lies in God's hands and His timing. It could be many days, months, or years between the time you receive a word and its reality. God's word is not invalid. We must learn to accept God's timing.

A friend of mine, who happens to be ordained through my ministry, received a prophetic word in 2005 that she would work full time with a particular ministry. Over the course of the next three years, many things happened that made it look like the complete opposite was true. In 2008, after a season of prayer, God led her to separate from that ministry and move on.

She did not understand how moving on could possibly bring about God's prophetic promise to her, but she obeyed. Over the next two years, God rearranged situations and circumstances to prepare a way so His original word to her could be fulfilled.

Following God's direction in faith put her in position to launch a new job in the ministry God had promised her. If she had stayed in 2008, rather than leaving as God instructed her, she would not have been in position to do what God needed her to do in 2010. Her difficult circumstances became the catalyst for her transition into full-time work with this ministry.

She did experience the fulfillment of the prophetic word she was given from God in 2005, but it did not come as she expected. In fact, it required her willingness to trust the leading of the Spirit, even when He led her away from her intended goal.

God may take you down a path you do not expect, but He will always bring you to the land of promise if you follow Him obediently. If you do not see the manifestation right away, do not give up. Rely on God. His word will be fulfilled in your life at the right time. God is never late. He knows every step your life will take and has a plan for getting you where He wants you. You can trust Him and follow His leading or you can choose to worry and never see your promise fulfilled. Your role with a prophetic word is faith and surrender to the leading of God's Spirit.

Take a moment now and consider God's promises for your life. Think about a prophetic word that you have received but have not yet seen fulfilled. If you have felt discouraged and full of doubt about it, take a moment and say this prayer:

Father, I thank You for the prophetic word You have given me for my life. I know sometimes I have doubted it would ever happen. I have even questioned if I really heard from You. Father, I ask You to forgive me for doubt and unbelief. I declare now, Father, that You are Lord over my life and that any word You have given me, any plan You have for me, will come to pass as I trust in You and walk in obedience to the leading of Your Holy Spirit. I thank You and I affirm my faith and my complete trust in You to bring it about in Your timing. In Jesus' name. Amen.

CHAPTER 5

Prophetic Faith

The role of faith in the prophetic ministry is not singular in nature. Faith requires other ingredients working with it to bring about the manifestation of the promises and prophecies of the Lord. In the prophetic sense, faith requires action and obedience.

ACTION

Many prophetic words come about due to the supernatural activity of God and the angelic realms around you working tirelessly. Some words are contingent on your action and obedience. Prophetic words come with direction and require action on your part. The book of James tells us about faith in action:

What good is it, my brothers and sisters, if someone claims to have faith but has no deeds? Can such faith save them? Suppose a brother or a sister is without clothes and daily food. If one of you says to them, "Go in peace; keep warm and well fed," but does nothing about their physical needs, what good is it? In the same way, faith by itself, if it is not accompanied by action, is dead.

But someone will say, "You have faith; I have deeds."

Show me your faith without deeds, and I will show you my faith by my deeds. You believe that there is one God. Good! Even the demons believe that—and shudder.

You foolish person, do you want evidence that faith without deeds is useless? Was not our father Abraham considered righteous for what he did when he offered his son Isaac on the altar? You see that his faith and his actions were working together, and his faith was made complete by what he did. And the Scripture was fulfilled that says, "Abraham believed God, and it was credited to him as righteousness," and he was called God's friend. You see that a person is considered righteous by what they do and not by faith alone. (James 2:14–24)

You can receive a prophetic word and believe that God will bring it about, but you must also act on your faith as the Spirit of God leads you. You may not always feel like acting. You may have to push yourself to take that first step. But once you take that first step and the next step, you will soon see that you are headed in the right direction. It may not always be fun, but as you walk out your faith, you will see the manifestation of God's will for your life.

For example, if you're looking for a job and a prophetic word tells you, "Go apply for a job at XYZ Company," what is the first thing you should do? Go to that company and apply for that job. Not filling out the job application form will keep you from your promise, the job you've been looking for. Push through the doubt, get up, and go! Once you have that new job, you will be glad you listened and acted on His direction.

God wants to bless you. He wants to bring about His promises in your life. But you have to be willing to do your part to work with Him to bring them into reality. It is not just a matter of praying, decreeing, or speaking words of faith. Those things are important, but Scripture says, "Faith without works is dead" (James 2:20 NKJV). You have to act in obedience as you make the decrees and walk by faith.

How does this work? If you receive a prophetic word that says, "If you take this action, God will do this on your behalf," your focus cannot be on the benefits of obedience until you act in faith. Many people want the blessing without the responsibility of obedience. This is simply laziness. God does not reward laziness, but obedience.

The Word of God says, "Work hard and become a leader; be lazy and become a slave" (Proverbs 12:24 NLT). Those who work hard will receive their reward, the promise, while those who are lazy will become slaves to their circumstances. Do you want to be a slave to debt? Do you want to be forced to work? If not, choose to be diligent, and put action to your faith. Create an opportunity for God's promises to manifest in your life.

If God delivers a prophetic word that you will write books that will go around the world, those books are not going to write themselves. You have to discipline yourself, set aside time to write, take action by sitting down and physically putting those words on paper. If you do not know how to type, you can record yourself speaking or teaching and have someone transcribe and edit that content for you. Either way, action is required on your part in order to bring about the manifestation of God's word for your life.

What has God spoken to you about your life that you have not seen come about yet? Are there things you need to be doing in order to bring about the fulfillment of that word for your life? If so, what are you waiting for? Repent of your procrastination, ask the Holy Spirit to help you, and get busy doing your part to bring about the promises of God for your life.

OBEDIENCE

Just as taking action is a crucial part of seeing the manifestation of God's prophetic word, obedience is also important. God's Word is filled with promises and prophetic words from God to His children. Many of these promises are conditional on obedience. You have to obey His instructions to get His benefits. We see this demonstrated in Scripture. Let's examine one of these biblical scenarios.

> Joshua summoned the Reubenites, the Gadites and the half-tribe of Manasseh and said to them, "You have done all that Moses the servant of the Lord commanded, and you have obeyed me in everything I commanded. For a long time now—to this very day—you have not deserted your fellow Israelites but have carried out the mission the Lord your God gave you. Now that the Lord your God has given them rest as he promised, return to your homes in the land that Moses the servant of the Lord gave you on the other side of the Jordan. But be very careful to keep the commandment and the law that Moses the servant

of the Lord gave you: to love the Lord your God, to walk in obedience to him, to keep his commands, to hold fast to him and to serve him with all your heart and with all your soul." (Joshua 22:1–5)

Three things transpire in this passage. First, Joshua acknowledges to the tribes that they had not only been careful to obey the commandments of God, but they were also careful to obey the commands given by Moses and Joshua, God's appointed leaders. Second, the result of this obedience was the fulfillment of God's promise, and their reward was the land God had planned for the tribes to inhabit. Finally, we see an exhortation from Joshua encouraging them to continue loving God, keeping His commands, and walking in obedience to Him.

In an earlier chapter of this book, I mentioned that prophecy can be described as a word that exhorts or encourages. Look at how Joshua delivers this message to the tribes. In Joshua 22, we see elements of exhortation and encouragement woven into his message. This was a prophetic proclamation to the twelve tribes of Israel. The promises of God were fulfilled because of their obedience to God.

Another profound example of blessings following obedience is found in Deuteronomy 28. I encourage you to read and meditate on the entire chapter to understand the relationship between obedience and blessing. Then examine the following Scriptures to see what happens when we obey.

It shall come to pass, if you diligently obey the voice of the Lord your God, to observe carefully all His commandments which I command you today, that the Lord your God will set you high above all nations of the earth. And all these blessings shall come upon you and overtake you, because you obey the voice of the Lord your God:

Blessed shall you be in the city, and blessed shall you be in the country.

Blessed shall be the fruit of your body, the produce of your ground and the increase of your herds, the increase of your cattle and the offspring of your flocks.

Blessed shall be your basket and your kneading bowl.

Blessed shall you be when you come in, and blessed shall you be when you go out.

The Lord will cause your enemies who rise against you to be defeated before your face; they shall come out against you one way and flee before you seven ways. The Lord will command the blessing on you in your storehouses and in all to which you set your hand, and He will bless you in the land which the Lord your God is giving you.

The Lord will establish you as a holy people to Himself, just as He has sworn to you, if you keep the commandments of the Lord your God and walk in His ways. (Deuteronomy 28:1–9 NJKV)

This list includes only a few of the benefits of obedience mentioned in Scripture. The chapter goes on to discuss some additional benefits and then concludes with the consequences for disobedience. If you look through those verses, you will see that it is always better to walk in obedience.

If you look at this scriptural example of the benefits of obedience to God's Word, you will see the same interactive process with the prophetic word. If God gives you a prophetic word that implies or directly instructs certain actions, then following through in obedience will make it possible for God to manifest the blessings that He promised.

The next chapter will explain some key elements to obedience as you walk out the prophetic word God has given you for your life.

CHAPTER 6

Key Components to Obedience

Just as real faith demands action and obedience, it also requires understanding of how God functions within a lifestyle of obedience. This will lead you to cooperate with the work of God in your life and understand how He works through hearing His voice, confirmation, preparation, timing, and walking out your prophetic destiny through obedience.

CONFIRMATION

I am going to make a statement that some people may disagree with, but I believe to be true. God is not obligated to confirm or repeat His word. If He has said something, then it is done. His word is all you need to know in order to walk in obedience. When God speaks and you respond with faith, action and obedience follow. He is not obligated to confirm or repeat His word, but He often does for our sake. Sometimes this is out of compassion for us and our human predisposition to question what we have heard. Sometimes He does this to give us a gentle nudge to follow the guidance He has already placed in our hearts.

Divinely inspired prophetic words will confirm what God is already telling you. He may use a word to confirm something He has shown you because you are not listening or accepting what He said to you. In these cases, God may use someone else to speak to you. This is His loving way of saying, "You heard Me. I will say it again. Now, do your part and I will keep My promise."

When you mature enough as a believer that you can distinguish God's voice from your own and no longer need somebody else to confirm what you hear from God, you can walk out your prophetic destiny in faith. Even mature believers appreciate a prophecy and will seek God's confirmation within their hearts before they fully receive it.

My daughter Melody used to joke, "I need to see a burning bush that is not consumed. I need a hand to write it on the wall so God can confirm His sign." She was in a place in her life where she needed confirmation of the confirmation of the confirmation! I have watched her grow and mature over the years. Now my heart fills with joy when I hear her say, "God, if You tell me to do something and put it on my heart, I will be obedient to Your direction. You do not have to speak through somebody else. You can talk directly to me and I will listen to You." This is a sign of true maturity.

A few years ago, our team held a prophetic healing and dream interpretation weekend. The prophet asked, "Who is under the age of thirty?" My daughter Melody and another man in the room were the only ones who raised their hands. The prophet said, "Sir, put your hand down. This word applies to anyone who has been under the age of thirty within the last three years." It was a specific word for a specific purpose.

Melody walked forward in obedience. The prophet put her hand on Melody's shoulder and said, "New job! New job! New job!"

Melody told me later that every time the prophet said, "New job," she said, "No way." At the time, she was living in Nashville, Tennessee. She liked traveling part time with the Joan Hunter Ministries and helping from Nashville while enjoying her life there. God had seen her faithfulness and wanted to elevate her into the calling that He had on her life by giving her more responsibility in the ministry.

The lease on her Nashville apartment would expire in October, but God told her to move to Houston in August. He said, "In the next six months you will be doing something completely different." He did not say, "Get a new job tomorrow." There was no surprise when the time arrived because she already knew God was leading her in a new direction.

She went from doing massage therapy and taking care of her sister's children in Nashville, Tennessee, to full-time ministry in Texas. She often reminds the ministry staff that she loves them all, but she would not trade them for her nieces and nephews. Melody loves spending time with those children. God makes sure her desire for quality time with the kids is satisfied even if her purpose in life is not to care for her nieces and nephews. She has to fulfill the call of God on her life.

When you surrender your heart to God, He will make sure all of your desires are met. He will make it possible for you to enjoy those things that you desire the most.

When God directs you down a new path, He wants you where

He can use you in a greater way than you are currently experiencing. When God told my daughter she was going to get a new job, she could have replied, "But I already work for the ministry." God was giving her an opportunity to have a voice within Joan Hunter Ministries. When she responded to that call, walked in obedience, and took the step of faith to make the move, God began to open new avenues and opportunities that she would not have had in Nashville. Without moving to Texas, she never would have chosen to be more involved in the ministry, nor would she have discovered how much God could use her to change the lives of others.

Her willingness to say, "I will accept this new assignment," allowed God to open up a whole new area of ministry for her. It brought a release of His anointing and kingdom promotion.

Are you willing to ask, "God, are You leading me in a new direction? Are You asking me to move? If You are, when do You want me to go? I do not want to go too soon or wait too long."

TIMING

It is important to understand God's timing. In Melody's story, His timing was of crucial importance. God prepared her heart in advance, notifying her that the move was coming. He spoke to her even when she did not want to obey His direction. It is a beautiful example of God's love and compassion that He would tell her in advance. He gave her time to accept the change and prepare for the transition He was about to bring into her life.

Another great example is in 1 Samuel 16, where Samuel anointed David and prophesied that he would become the king of Israel. David did not go to the palace and put on the crown immediately after being anointed with oil by God's prophet. Instead, he went right back to the field to care for the sheep.

Put that into the context of your present-day experience. Suppose a prophet says you are going to be the next president of the United States, but you lack the experience of political office. After receiving the word, you go back to washing dishes, scrubbing tables, and serving coffee because the word is meant for the future.

David could have said, "If God is really making me king, I should be doing that right now instead of taking care of sheep." But David understood that God's word was not for the present. So he returned to what he knew and waited for the spirit of God to lead him and open the door for him to gain control of the throne.

Even when David did enter the king's court, he did not charge in and proclaim that God had anointed him as the next king. Rather, he served the present king faithfully until God elevated him to the throne and fulfilled the prophecy that Samuel had given him years before when he was a shepherd in his father's house.

Take a closer look at the scenario in 1 Samuel 16 where Samuel finds David and anoints him as the next king.

So it was, when they came, that he looked at Eliab and said, "Surely the Lord's anointed is before Him!" But the Lord said to Samuel, "Do not look at his appearance or at his physical stature, because I have refused him. For the Lord does not see as man sees; for man looks at the outward appearance, but the Lord looks at the heart." (1 Samuel16:6–7 NKJV)

Samuel evaluated each son of Jesse, who would have made a great leader based on his physical or intellectual attributes.

One by one, Jesse's seven sons approached Samuel and were all rejected. They were not acceptable to God's purposes.

God said of each of these men, "His outside appearance is not what will make him a great king. What is more important, and what will see him through the challenges faced by a king, is what is in his heart, combined with his ability to listen and be guided by Me."

Then Samuel asked, "Are these all the sons you have?"

"There is still the youngest," Jesse replied. "But he's out in the fields watching the sheep and goats."

"Send for him at once," Samuel said. "We will not sit down to eat until he arrives."

So Jesse sent for him. He was dark and handsome, with beautiful eyes.

And the Lord said, "This is the one; anoint him."

So as David stood there among his brothers, Samuel took the flask of olive oil he had brought and anointed David with the oil. And the Spirit of the Lord came powerfully upon David from that day on. (1 Samuel16:11–13 NLT)

David was a shepherd, and he understood the need for the sheep to listen to his voice. While tending sheep, David learned by personal experience what God's heart was like. He learned how to watch over, protect, and lead the sheep. He needed this ability to rule as king. Because he learned to listen to God's voice and follow Him, he was able to lead the people of Israel where God wanted to take them.

God is looking for a group of people to use for His purposes. He wants to say prophetically, "These are My chosen ones, whom

I am sending. They will listen for My voice and be obedient to My will instead of thinking, *This is silly* or *This cannot be God, it must be just me.*"

Take time to study, understand, and develop the ability to hear God and speak His prophetic word into other people's lives. What if Samuel had not listened to God and obeyed Him? What if Samuel had anointed the son he thought would be the best king instead of anointing David, as God instructed? The story would have had a much different ending.

Outward appearances do not impress God. He does not see things the same way you and I do. He does not see through human eyes. His wisdom is beyond human intelligence and His vision is fixed in eternity.

HEARING

As you learn to hear God's voice, you will not only receive the word of the Lord and His direction for your own life, but you can share that revelation with others as well.

Not long ago, I felt the spirit of God move on my heart to share a word with a friend of mine. I sent her a message, saying, "I really believe that God is calling you into something new and different. I am not trying to be super-spiritual, but I just feel like I should tell you this." She confirmed that I was correct when she said, "Thank you. This agrees with what God has already shown me."

When God gives insight or revelation to you regarding a situation, do not classify it as strange and discard it. Instead, when you realize it is a word that would exhort, comfort, and speak life to another person, step out of your comfort zone and be bold. Send a text message or make a phone call. Encourage that person with whatever God has revealed to you. As you practice releasing what He is giving you, the gift will continue to grow, develop, and become more precise.

David was not seeking a prophetic word. He did not search for Samuel to ask, "What does God have for my life?" David was where he was supposed to be. He was faithful to do what God had put in front of him for that season. When it was time for God to get a message to him, He sent a prophet to deliver the word David needed to hear. Samuel did not deliver just any word, but a word that would change the direction of David's entire future.

When it was time for the fulfillment of His word, God arranged circumstances to fulfill that word. David just had to believe, obey, and act when God told him to act. He had to follow God's voice and remain in His timing.

Sometimes it's not easy to hear the voice of God. With all the noise, distractions, and stressors in life, God's voice can seem muffled or faint. Other times, when you seek God, your prayers may seem to bounce off the ceiling and not reach God's ears. In these times, ask God to point you in the right direction. He may need to give you a compass to guide you down the path He has chosen for you.

When my daughter Melody was in her twenties, she was struggling to figure out God's path for her life. She prayed and prayed. Finally, she said, "God, I am going to give You my all. But You have to give me a place to begin and tell me what You are going to do. You've told me You have a purpose for my life, but I need You to give me some inkling of the plan You have for me. I need You to speak to me."

One day, she went to a church where an awesome revival was being held. Dr. Christian Harfouche said, "Somebody here has low back pain." Being around the healing ministry all her life,

Melody knew, statistically, out of the approximately one thousand people present, chances were that many people would raise their hands. To her surprise, she was the only person who came forward. When the minister prayed for her, God healed her back.

But that is not all that happened.

He then delivered a prophetic word to her: "You have stepped into the cocoon of the anointing that is your inheritance." He had no idea who she was. He did not know I was her mom or that Charles and Frances Hunter were her grandparents. He did not have any idea what her inheritance would be. Because Melody was willing to let everything go and be obedient to what God had called her to do, God gave her a clue to what He had planned for her life. It was a season where God was protecting and developing her before bringing her into the new life He had for her.

Melody had not received many prophetic words at that point, but this one stuck with her because it was such a life-defining moment and a direct answer to prayer. She had been seeking direction for her life and God delivered!

I encourage you to step into the cocoon of your anointing and become the new creature God has called you to be.

CHAPTER 7

Prophetic Intimacy with God

God would rather speak to you directly than through someone else.

God's original plan for humanity was for all men to walk in intimacy with Him every day of their lives. When Adam and Eve were in the garden of Eden, God took great delight in walking with Adam in the "cool of the day" (Genesis 3:8), spending quality time with Him. God desired this kind of fellowship and communion with man from the moment of creation.

Unfortunately, the fall of man caused a separation between the Creator and His creation. For several thousand years, God was limited to speaking through His prophets. He still longed to be in loving communion with His beloved creation, but sin kept God from being able to have that full access to humanity.

Before Jesus came to remove the barrier between man and

God, the only way for God to commune with man was through His priests and prophets. It was primarily secondhand communication, unfulfilling and incomplete.

In Old Testament times, the presence of God was contained behind a thick veil inside the temple, a place called the "holy of holies." Only the high priest had permission to enter at specific times of the year to access the presence of God on behalf of the people. When Jesus died on the cross, this veil of separation was torn and God's presence was made available to mankind through that ultimate sacrifice.

> After Jesus cried out again in a loud voice, he died. At that moment the temple curtain was torn in two from top to bottom. The earth shook. The rocks split. Tombs broke open. The bodies of many holy people who had died were raised to life. They came out of the tombs. After Jesus was raised from the dead, they went into the holy city. There they appeared to many people. (Matthew 27:50–53 NIRV)

God was so eager to restore a relationship with man that the first thing He did when Jesus died was to destroy the veil that separated Him from mankind. This act demonstrates how much He longs for and desires intimacy with His children: you and me. He loves you and wants an intimate relationship with you. He wants you to have access to Him. He does not want to speak to you through a priest or through a prophet. He prefers to speak to you directly, face to face and heart to heart.

When I read this Scripture, I envision God's heart breaking as He turned His face away from His beloved Son. Yet He knew that as soon as Jesus gave up His spirit, the loving relationship between God and all of His creation would be restored. I imagine Him sitting on the throne, waiting for the exact moment when He would issue the command to destroy the veil. No longer would God be separated from His children.

Jesus' blood paid the price so you and I can go into that most holy place and communicate with Him directly. When you understand the magnitude of His love for you, you will never again doubt His desire to speak directly to you.

By tearing the veil, God was saying, "You can come see Me. Through Jesus' sacrifice, we can talk to each other without a third party involved." Intimate communication was the goal God always intended for our lives. You can hear directly from God. You can also be a conduit or connection for revelation to others through prophetic ministry.

If you want to prophesy to others, pray, "God, give me the words to encourage, strengthen, and edify people." If you spend time with God and humbly share His messages with others, He will give you more opportunities to minister His word.

The key to receiving prophetic words is to deliver them when He tells you to do so. God will not give you prophetic words if you stack them in the back of a filing cabinet and leave them there. When God gives you prophetic words, you have to deliver them. Each time you deliver His messages, you make room for more.

Sometimes, after delivering a prophetic message to someone, I can't recall exactly what I said. However, I do remember the messages that apply to me, even if I was the one who spoke the words.

Don't be concerned if you don't remember the prophecy you delivered to another. You are the conduit from God and are simply repeating His message.

Seek God for Your Own Word

Because I flow in the prophetic, I give and receive prophetic words regularly. I have no problem delivering words to others. In fact, I enjoy it very much. But I encourage you to seek God for wisdom before seeking a man to be His messenger to you. God wants to speak to you directly. Before you seek a prophetic word from a human being, seek Him.

"Seek first his kingdom and his righteousness, and all these things will be given to you as well" (Matthew 6:33).

If you want to prophesy, seek God's face and get to know His Word. The Bible contains all the answers you are seeking as well as the life-giving power you need.

It is time for the body of Christ to rise up in the power and authority of Jesus Christ and become mature in the things of the Spirit. You have the same access to God that I have. You have the same access to God that your pastor has. You have the same access to God as your favorite prophet. Do not let the enemy lie to you and tell you otherwise. God wants to talk to you, He wants to speak through you, and He wants to use you directly. The only question is this: Are you willing to take the time to invest in a close relationship with Him as much as you invest in your relationships with other people or your favorite television show? Where are your priorities?

As you spend time reading and studying the Bible, you will become intimately familiar with God, and His voice will become clear to you. Do you want to hear from God more often? Get in the Word! Do you want God to speak through you to others? Do you want to be used in the ministry of prophecy? Spend time with the one you want to know. Spend time with the one who wants to use your voice.

The prophetess who gave my daughter Melody a word about a new job spends more time in the Word than anyone I know. I've seen her sitting on her luggage in airports, devouring the Word of God and flipping pages as if her life were on the line. She understands that there is life-giving power in the Word of God. She devours it and consumes it. His Word is part of her DNA.

Because of her commitment and hunger for the things of God and the power of His word active in her life, her prophetic words are very precise. It is as if God puts a microphone to her mouth when He speaks through her to others. One specific prophecy after another flow from her lips like water flows from a brook. Why is it so easy for her to receive and share prophetic words? Because she spends so much time with God, seeking His kingdom through the study of His Word. She knows Him, and He speaks to her and through her.

God wants to speak to you too. He craves your heart, your time, and your attention. He desires to spend intimate moments with you. He wants to speak to your heart about your life and the direction He is taking you. Will you let Him? Will you give Him the time?

Melody's Experiences

It has been a joy to watch my daughter Melody grow and develop in prophetic ministry. I asked her to share some examples of her experiences in this book. The following paragraphs are in her words.

When I first started flowing in the prophetic and allowing God to speak through me to others, I was traveling a lot with my ministry. But whenever I was in town, I attended a church pastored by Marcus Davis, who was one of my coworkers. As a friend and I were pulling into the church parking lot that morning, there was a car in front of me. I felt God was giving me a word for the driver, a person I didn't know. I was not sure when or how I was to deliver this word, but I knew God always has a perfect way.

We went into church and sat down. Pastor Marcus spoke for a while and then said, "I believe God wants to share a specific word with those who are here today. Does anybody have a word?"

I certainly did not think he was talking about me. So I continued worshipping as Pastor Sheila played on the keyboard.

Suddenly I remembered the word I had received in the parking lot. I wondered if I was supposed to share this word.

My friend whispered, "It's you, isn't it?"

"Yes," I admitted.

But I was hesitant. I didn't want to grab a microphone and start ministering or giving prophetic words like my mother, Joan Hunter, or my grandparents, Charles and Frances Hunter. I just wanted to go to church and worship God and receive from His Word that day.

Pastor Marcus was not going to let it go. He repeated, "God has given somebody here a word for this morning."

I breathed a sigh of relief when another woman in the congregation said, "I have a word."

Even though I knew God wanted me to give the word He had given me, I thought, *Awesome! She will give it. I don't have to say anything.*

The woman shared a Scripture. It was a good word. Scripture is always inspiring. But it did not really speak to me. And it did not match the word God had told me to release.

When she finished, Pastor Marcus said, "I really believe that God has given somebody a specific word for this morning, and we are going to stay right here until the Holy Spirit moves and releases this word."

Knowing that I was not going to get off the hook, I stood. Pastor Marcus said, "Let me get the microphone for you."

He hadn't given the other lady a microphone. This was exactly what I did not want to happen.

He handed me the microphone and said, "Here you go."

I gave the word that God had given me when I arrived in the parking lot. I had initially thought it was for the woman who was in front of my car when I pulled in. But as I delivered it, God revealed that it was a word that applied corporately, and many people present that day were able to receive from it.

That was the first time, in all my years of going to church and being in that kind of environment, that I received a word from God to deliver corporately. And it was very exciting! Even though I was not looking to be "that kind of person," God chose to use me in that way. And He allowed my pastor to be sensitive enough to the move of His Spirit to wait until I was willing to share.

The following week, I happened to be in town again on Sunday and was able to go to the same church. As we were worshipping, Pastor Marcus said, "I really believe that the Holy Spirit has given us a word this morning." Then he said, "I am going to wait right here and let the Holy Spirit move and deliver the word as He has given it to you."

Nope, I thought, *it's not me this time. God wouldn't give me prophetic words two weeks in a row, right? That's not how He does things.*

Another person came forward and gave a word. Afterward, Pastor Marcus stood in the middle of the aisle, waiting. Finally he made eye contact with me and said, "I believe God has given you a specific word to share. Even though you shared a word last week, God has given you a word for today."

I just stood there, staring at him. And I had an epiphany. Ding, ding, ding! *Okay, I get it, God!*

This time, I was more comfortable with what God wanted me to do. I shared a word He had given me earlier in the week, which I had also shared with our ministry staff. It was such a powerful word that I wanted to release it over the people in the congregation.

I also want to share this word with you. God's word is not constrained by time or location. The same word I released that day at church can apply to your situation today. Here is the message God gave me:

"There are puzzle pieces lying around. Because something is keeping you from seeing the pieces clearly, you have no idea how the edges will fit, or even if the pieces will make the puzzle come together. In the next six months, the timing of this word will be completed. God is bringing things into play and into position on your behalf so you will see how the pieces connect. It will not be as hard as you thought it would be because He is the one who will move and shift the pieces. It is similar to the tectonic plates deep within the earth that bump together and cause earthquakes. That is how dramatically these pieces will come together. You will feel things come into alignment and fit together the way they are supposed to."

After I delivered this word to the congregation at my church, I told them to receive it if it applied to them. If it was not for them, just thank God that it applied to somebody else.

When I gave the microphone back to Pastor Marcus, he said, "Church, in the last several weeks, we have met with many people who were trying to figure out what God is showing them, where He is taking them, and how He is going to work things out. If this word applies to you in any way, I want you to stand up."

To my surprise, only two people remained sitting. More than forty people received the word as confirmation that God was repositioning them and moving on their behalf to put things together.

When God asked me to share that word corporately, I could easily have convinced myself that God would not use me two weeks in a row to share a word. I could have been concerned about what people in the church would think. *Oh, that's just Joan's daughter trying to take over the microphone again.* I was indeed reluctant to share a word because I was worried how others would feel about me. Instead I chose to trust God when He said, "You need to give this word."

I'm glad I pushed aside my concerns and was obedient to God. If I had not obeyed, two things would have happened. First, the people who needed that encouraging word would not have received it and would have left church that day still wondering about God's direction and path for their lives. Second, I would have been walking in disobedience by withholding a word God wanted delivered. I would have blocked the flow of new words He wanted me to deliver in the future. God cannot give you new assignments until you complete the ones He has already given you.

From this experience I learned that when God gives you a word, it might be for more than one person or group of people. I delivered it to my ministry staff first. Later, He wanted to deliver it to my church. And now He is giving it to you through this book. If it applies to you, receive it.

God's word may take on a slightly different look and feel as He delivers it to various audiences. If a prophetic word is different each time you deliver it, that's OK. God always gives a fresh word specifically designed for the person or people receiving it.

Through this particular word I received and delivered, God was saying to His children, "Set the pieces down, take a step back, and allow Me to move." If you look at a thousand-piece puzzle that needs to be assembled, you may feel completely overwhelmed. However, if you take a step back and get an idea of what the finished picture should look like, you can identify the edge pieces you didn't see before. You can sort the pieces into colors and sections. Pieces will finally come together and then the total picture will come alive.

One of the things my mother shares in her teachings is that we need to see God's perspective in all situations. Take that step back and say, "God, give me Your perspective on this. Show me what You are doing and how I fit into this situation." It seems so simple. Indeed, this approach is both simple and effective. If you ask God to show you, He will.

I encourage you to say to God, "However the pieces need to fall, I trust You will put them into place in a way that I cannot. I know You can and will make it work." When you trust God enough to take your hands off the situation, step back, and let Him work it out, you will see how miraculously the pieces of your life come together. As our ministry team often says, "Miracles happen not by our hand, but by God's. We are just vessels for Him to flow through."

CHAPTER 8

Stewardship of the Prophetic Word

*T*he Scriptures are filled with prophetic words for you, as well as instruction on how to apply the words you receive and see the fulfillment of God's promises for your life. Essentially, results come down to your stewardship of the words you receive, whether through a Scripture, a divine revelation, or a direct spoken word.

Take a moment to examine what a few Scriptures say about prophecy:

"Pursue love, and desire spiritual gifts, but especially that you may prophesy" (1 Corinthians 14:1 NKJV).

"For you can all prophesy one by one, that all may learn and all may be encouraged" (1 Corinthians 14:31 NKJV).

"I will hear what God the Lord will speak, for He will
speak peace to His people and to His saints; but let them
not turn back to folly" (Psalm 85:8 NKJV).

Many people think of prophetic ministry as a form of judgment, doom and gloom. Indeed, some prophecy is intended
to correct. If a prophetic person delivers correction with an
absence of love, the word can seem harsh and critical. However,
the gift of prophecy is intended to encourage and edify the body
of Christ.

Those operating in the gift of prophecy may sometimes have
to deliver a word of correction, but it can always be presented in
such a way that it does not discourage or condemn the person
or people receiving it. If God wants you to deliver a word of correction to someone, be sure to pray about how to deliver it. Ask
the Holy Spirit to help you present it in a way that will be well
received by the person so he or she will feel inspired and encouraged to make the necessary changes rather than condemned and
beat up by the message.

When I was first told I was to take on the role of a prophet,
I was tempted to run the opposite direction. I had heard many
prophets who were rough, tough, and downright nasty as they
verbally browbeat and whipped audiences with "words from
God." I did not want to do that. Talking that way is not my personality at all. I told God I would prophesy only if I could be a
sweet prophet instead of a nasty one.

Do not ever deliver a word from God with anger or condemnation. Even words of correction should be given with life, love,
and patience, the fruits of God's Spirit.

As God gives you messages to share with other people from
His heart of love and based on the word He has given you, He

will bring life to those words. It is not up to you to make anything happen. Your only responsibility is to be obedient in receiving and repeating the messages God gives you.

How to Handle
the Prophetic Words You Receive

There are six steps to the proper stewardship of a prophetic word. They are:

1. Write it down or record it in some other fashion.

2. Pray over it, judge it by Scripture, and confirm it in your heart.

3. Be obedient.

4. Remove strongholds that prevent the word from being fulfilled.

5. Wait patiently for the message to come to pass.

6. Continue to develop your character and integrity as a believer in God's Word.

Take a close look at each of these steps. How will you implement them in your life? Ask God to show you what to do, how to do it, and when.

Write It Down

When you receive a prophetic word, take a few moments to write it down as soon as possible. It may be convenient to record it on your smart phone or voice recorder. Try to document what God is giving you as soon as possible, or you may not remember it accurately. If someone is about to deliver a word to you, ask that person to wait until you prepare your phone to record the word. If you do not have a smart phone, perhaps someone nearby will record it for you. If you are in a meeting, and the hosting facility is recording the meeting, ask if you can get a copy of the recording.

A friend of mine has a journal dedicated to prophetic words she has received. She has found this to be an invaluable tool to refer to as situations or circumstances challenge her faith. She is able to go back to the journals and say, "On that date God made me this promise." Having these words recorded in one place has kept her standing on God's promises in the face of some trying and adverse circumstances.

Be Obedient

The Scriptures are filled with commands to walk in obedience to God's instruction. Obedience brings blessings on your life and facilitates the fulfillment of God's purposes, plans, and prophetic words. Your disobedience can delay or even abort a prophetic word delivered to you. Disobedience brings a curse of death; however, not necessarily physical death. Sometimes this is death to the promises of God for your life.

> "Listen to me. I'm setting a blessing and a curse in front of you today. I'm giving you the commands of the Lord your God today. You will be blessed if you obey them. But you will be cursed if you don't obey them. So don't turn away from the path I'm now commanding you to take. Don't turn away by worshiping other gods you didn't know before" (Deuteronomy 11:26–28 NIRV).

"Obey faithfully everything that I have commanded you, and all will go well for you and your descendants forever, because you will be doing what is right and what pleases the Lord your God" (Deuteronomy 12:28 GNT).

I exhort you to behave responsibly with the prophetic word you receive. Your response to God's instruction will affect your "descendants forever." Follow through with the required steps. To see the fulfillment of your prophetic word from God, be active in what you were instructed to do.

Remove Strongholds

Strongholds can be established in your life by the words you or others speak about you and your situation. It is important to break and remove the strongholds that can be a barrier to the fulfillment and manifestation of God's plans for you. How are they established? How do you remove them? The Scripture teaches us that there is power in our words.

"From the fruit of their mouth a person's stomach is filled; with the harvest of their lips they are satisfied. The tongue has the power of life and death, and those who love it will eat its fruit" (Proverbs 18:20–21).

You can and should stand guard over your own words and speak life into your situation, circumstance, or atmosphere. But you cannot control what others say about you. People in your life may be speaking against your success and dreams because they think God has called you to do something else. If this is happening, you may have to take action. Sometimes people need to be removed from your life or your environment for a season while God perfects His work within you.

You might not have to remove people from your life completely, but you may need to remove their voices from you. When they offer advice, you can say, "Right now I will trust the Holy Spirit. This is what He has called me to do. I will step forward into His calling, His plan, and His purpose."

If someone has spoken against you personally, or against the word and promises of God you have received, or your dreams for your future, you can break the power of those words over your life with a simple prayer like this:

Father, I have spoken words that did not edify, build up, or correct in love. I ask You to forgive me for those words. I cut their power off of my life in Jesus' name. Father, others have spoken words against me that did not edify, build up, or correct in love. I ask You to forgive them, and I cut the power of their words off of my life in Jesus' name. I am blessed, and I will walk into the fullness of everything You have for me in my life. Amen.

Strongholds can also come from faulty mind-sets, generational patterns, or programming from your life experiences. These can limit or prevent you from being able to fully believe and accept the word that God has given you. Strongholds can cause a delay or a block to fulfillment of the prophetic word in your life. Your thoughts and beliefs about yourself determine the course of your life. Proverbs talks about this.

"As he thinks in his heart, so is he" (Proverbs 23:7 NKJV).

"As water reflects the face, so one's life reflects the heart" (Proverbs 27:19).

Guard your prophetic word and the direction of your life as it relates to the word you have received from God. Ensure that your thought life matches the promises of God and that it supports what the Word of God says about you and what the prophetic word says about your future.

The renewing of your mind through the Word of God tears down the strongholds of the mind. Draw more of His Word into your heart and mind, then decree and declare that Word over your life to maximize the manifestations of His promises in your life.

"Do not conform to the pattern of this world, but be transformed by the renewing of your mind. Then you will be able to test and approve what God's will is—his good, pleasing and perfect will" (Romans 12:2).

Deal with the strongholds in your life and overcome them by the power of the Word of God and your faith in His ability to fulfill His promises to you. Remove the strongholds, and do not allow a negative attitude any place in your life. Do your part, and be assured that God will do His part!

Wait Patiently

When you receive a word from God, you do not know how long it will take for the word to come to pass. It could be a quick turn-around, but more often than not, it will appear in the future. God will sometimes give you "now words," which are for the present or the near future. But most of God's promises for your life will come wrapped in a preface of "wait."

Waiting can feel brutal at times. But it is not just waiting that matters, it is waiting patiently. Trust that the word of the Lord is going to appear in your life no matter how long it might take or what your circumstances may look like today.

Your attitude while you wait will affect the fulfillment of that word and can either speed it up or slow it down. If you have a bad attitude and do not want to do the necessary work to fulfill it, nothing may happen. You can make that word null and void because of your own actions of disobedience.

Wait on the Lord and realize that the wait will bring good things into your life. I love what Lamentations 3:25 (NASB) says: "The Lord is good to those who wait for Him."

I say to myself, "The Lord is my inheritance; therefore, I will hope in him!" The Lord is good to those who depend on him, to those who search for him. So it is good to wait quietly for salvation from the Lord. (Lamentations 3:24–26 NLT)

Charles Spurgeon, a great Christian writer and theologian, explained it this way:

"If the Lord Jehovah makes us wait, let us do so with our whole hearts; for blessed are all they that wait for Him. He is worth waiting for. The waiting itself is beneficial to us: it tries faith, exercises patience, trains submission, and endears the blessing when it comes. The Lord's people have always been a waiting people."[1]

Waiting on the Lord is not something to be dreaded, it is something to enjoy. Let your waiting be done with the excitement and anticipation of a child waiting for Christmas. Children know awesome gifts are waiting for them under the tree, but they

---

1 Charles Spurgeon, *The Treasury of David: An Original Exposition of the Book of Psalms* (New York: Funk & Wagnalls, 1886), 68.

also know they must wait for the proper time to receive and open those gifts. God is bringing good things into your life. Wait for them with eagerness, anticipation, and excitement.

Develop Your Character and Integrity

Take a step back and ask the Holy Spirit to reveal truth to you through Scripture. Then seek understanding so the Scripture will direct your paths. Psalm 119:105 confirms this: "Your word is a lamp for my feet, a light on my path."

As you read, study, and pursue the Word of God, He will illuminate the path in front of you and clearly reveal the path you should follow. The Word may not tell you which car to buy, whether or not to renew your lease, or where you should move. However, the more you read the Word, the more familiar you become with your Father and hearing His voice becomes easier. He will lead you as your path is illuminated by His Word.

HOW TO DISCERN
THE PROPHETIC WORD

When you receive a prophetic word for yourself or for someone else, discern or evaluate the word by asking yourself these questions:

1. Does this line up with the Word of God?

2. Does this exalt or lift up the name of Jesus?

3. Does this bring edification, exhortation, and comfort?

4. Does it line up with the scriptural purpose of prophecy?

5. Does the Holy Spirit confirm the word as you are hearing it?

Answering these questions should give you the necessary information to discern whether a word is from God. If the answers create resistance in your spirit, you may choose to reject the word. If you feel the Holy Spirit inside you say, "That word is not from Me," do not receive that word.

This is why it is so important to understand the Word of God, know what it says, and spend time with God through prayer. As you spend time with the Shepherd, you become more familiar with His voice and you'll know when it is Him talking to you and when it is the voice of another. You will recognize His voice when He speaks.

"My sheep hear my voice, and I know them, and they follow me" (John 10:27 KJV).

If the Holy Spirit inside you says, "This car is a lemon, do not buy it," or, "There are holes in the roof you do not see, don't sign that contract," pay attention! Obedience is an essential key to everything that God has for you, a factor you cannot ignore or erase.

Not every person who gives you a prophetic word is truly hearing from God for your life. Some people may think they are hearing from God, but they are simply sharing their own opinions or thoughts about your situation based on what they see with their eyes or hear with their ears. When you receive a word from anyone, ask God to confirm that the message is from Him.

Pray, "God, I trust You will speak through other people concerning my life, but is this particular word for me?" If it is, He will confirm it in your spirit and through Scripture. If the word you receive from someone does not line up with Scripture, you can know it was not from God. He will never tell you something that is not in alignment with His written Word. He will always confirm His word to you by Scripture and in your heart, and sometimes He will confirm it through another person.

To discern whether to accept or reject a word spoken to you, consider these questions:

1. Is the person well respected in the Christian community?

2. Does his or her life line up with the Word of God?

If you are planning to attend a meeting, check out the reputation and believability of the host organization and the featured speakers and/or prophets. But discernment is necessary no matter who gives you a word.

Most organizations are careful about who is allowed to speak a word or interpret Scripture. But when I receive a word outside of an organization-sponsored meeting, I am even more careful of words given by someone I don't know. If I don't feel the word is authentic, I immediately cut it off in Jesus' name.

Another way to discern the validity of a prophetic word is to recognize where the word is directing you. Is it pointing you to God or to a person? Prophecy should always draw people to God, not to any human being. As God develops the gift of prophecy in you, remember that your words should give life and speak life.

Allow God to confirm the word. If the person you are sharing with says, "I already felt like He was showing me this," that is your confirmation.

When you receive a word for someone else, you do not have to get confirmation from God before you share it with anyone.

Your job is to step out in faith to deliver the word God has given you and let the ones who receive it evaluate it.

You will go through seasons where you do not hear God as clearly as you would like. In these times God is testing your faith and revealing where you are in your walk with Him. God is not being mean by being silent. He is just letting you walk out what He knows you have inside you. You may have heard it said, "The teacher never talks during a test." In the same way, God may not speak when you are going through a difficult time.

In these seasons, you may need to hear somebody tell you that God is still in control and that He cares about your life. You want Him to explain things you do not understand. But this season is meant to draw you closer to God, not to a person giving you a word. Remember that God cares enough to hear your request and He will deliver a message to you.

A word given through you to someone else serves the dual purpose of drawing both of you closer to God. You hear His voice when the Holy Spirit is ministering through you.

When you ask God to speak to you, be willing to let Him speak in whatever way He wants to. He may give you a word through something you find lying on the floor. When that happens, you will know that God is communicating directly to you. Only you will understand what He is saying.

God can also speak through music. If a song plays over and over in your head, or you wake up with one on your heart, that may be God speaking life into you about a circumstance or situation you are in or one you are about to face.

Sara Bareilles performs a popular song called "Brave." When my daughter heard this song, she shared it with a group of individuals at one of our conferences. From this song, God gave her a prophetic word to release over the lives of the people who were present.

The lyrics to this song, although not Christian, hold a key to what believers need to do. Listening to them with a prophetic ear, you can hear God calling believers to stand up and say, "This is not a religious opinion or something to be ignored."

God wants you to speak up. Ask Him for the ability, a voice, and an opportunity to be heard. When you receive the word, speak it without fear of what others may say or think. No one can censor what God wants to do in and through your life. Speak up, and take every opportunity to be brave for God.

CHAPTER 9

Prophecy: What It Is and What It Is Not

In a nutshell, prophesying is the process of speaking for God in a situation. Prophesying is not preaching or teaching.

An important part of empowering others in ministry is training them to hear God, whether for themselves or for another's situation. Our team is trained not to preach or deliver long teachings when they minister to people. The goal of ministry is to hear God's voice and share what He says. Most of the time, God will give you something that is relatively brief but personal.

Just because something is true and good does not make it the appropriate thing for you to say. You may have many good ideas, but the point of prophetic ministry is sharing what God says, not your opinions. If you have not yet learned the difference, ask God to help you grow and develop in this area.

Take time to listen to what He instructs you to do without adding anything else. Your opinion about another's problem or situation should not be part of your prophecy to him or her. Delivering the word of the Lord to someone is not about tickling that person's ears. The word should be delivered in kindness, not with tempting entertainment.

An ongoing fascination for people today is speculation on biblical prophecies concerning the end times. Speculation does not produce much in the way of godly fruit, but it can produce irrational human behavior. Delivering the word of the Lord is not for speculation or telling people what you think they want to hear. Jesus said that He could only do what He saw or heard the Father doing (John 5:19). Jesus is our example in all things. If He did only what the Father told Him to do, then we should operate the same way.

Prophesying is not fortune-telling. A person who prophesies is not a vending machine. You do not put a quarter in a prophet and get a word from God in return. A real prophetic word comes from God and is then shared with the intended person. It is not something from the prophet's spirit or flesh to deliver "on demand." It is best if the prophet has time to pray over a word before delivering it.

The more seasoned a person becomes in the prophetic, the more accurately he or she hears God and the less time is needed to pray over it. There is a fine balance here, because delivering a word to someone needs to be done in God's timing. You do not want to take too long to pray over something or the word may lose its impact by being delivered too late.

People are hungry for a word from God. The best-case

scenario for every believer is to be trained and equipped to receive directly from God for himself. It is great to receive a word from another person, but these words should always be for confirmation of something God has already been telling you.

Before you seek a word, ask these important questions:

1. Do you want a word from God?

2. Are you struggling and need His direction?

3. Are you willing to do whatever He tells you to do?

4. Are you willing to do it when and how He tells you to?

5. Are you willing to go wherever He tells you to go?

If you answered no to any of those questions, that could be why you are not hearing from God.

God continually moves us to new places, in new directions, and into things outside our comfort zone. He colors outside the lines we draw for ourselves. God has His own design for your life that may not match up with yours. His plan is always better!

In Ephesians 6:17, the Word of God is described as the sword of the Spirit, not the cotton swab of the Spirit. Hebrews 4:12 says that this sword divides the soul from the spirit. Do not be surprised if you feel a little pain from time to time when you receive a word. That does not mean the person prophesying has a problem with you or is unkind. It just means the word you are receiving is doing its job within you.

Some things are inappropriate when you prophesy. When you are ministering, preaching, teaching, prophesying, or healing, the pulpit is not the place to vent your anger or frustration at other people's behavior. Ministry is not an avenue to settle personal differences or "straighten out" people. Ministry time is for delivering God's message to the people, not your message.

If you are angry, go to your prayer closet and stay there until you get rid of that spirit. The Bible says, "If you become angry, do not let your anger lead you into sin, and do not stay angry all day" (Ephesians 4:26 GNT).

No good fruit comes from an outburst of anger. In most cases, an expression of anger toward a person results in more conflict and drives a wedge in the relationship.

"My dear brothers and sisters, take note of this: Everyone should be quick to listen, slow to speak and slow to become angry, because human anger does not produce the righteousness that God desires" (James 1:19–20).

Even if your anger is justified, it will not achieve the goals God has for you or the other person. Your anger will not produce righteousness in someone else. Romans 2:4 teaches that the kindness of God leads a person to repentance, not anger or judgment.

When you are ministering or delivering a prophetic word, That is not the time to publicly correct someone for wrong behavior. Matthew 18:15–17 (NIRV) says:

If your brother or sister sins against you, go to them. Tell them what they did wrong. Keep it between the two of you. If they listen to you, you have won them back. But what if they won't listen to you? Then take one or two others with you. Scripture says, "Every matter must be proved by the words of two or three witnesses." (Deuteronomy 19:15) But what if they also refuse to listen to the witnesses? Then tell it to the church. And what if they refuse to listen even to the church? Then don't treat them as a brother or sister. Treat them as you would treat an ungodly person or a tax collector.

Why did Jesus say to treat misbehaving believers as pagans, Gentiles, or tax collectors? During biblical times, the Jewish people used the word *dog* to describe Gentiles, which was as low of an insult as you could get. The tax collector was a Jewish person who collected money from his brethren to give to the Romans. He was considered lower than a dog.

Ecclesiastes 3:1–8 says there is a time and a season for all things. But from the pulpit or during personal ministry is not the place to correct others. If all you want is for God to bless the decisions you have already made, you do not need a prophetic word. If you have already made up your mind, you do not need Him, and He will not intervene in your life. If you are looking for a word on a previous decision, you are out of alignment with God and will not be able to hear what He says to you.

When prophesying or ministering to someone, it is not your responsibility to make the word of God come to pass. You are only to deliver the word, then let God do the work.

"I know whom I have believed, and am convinced that he is able to guard what I have entrusted to him until that day" (2 Timothy 1:12).

"We have different gifts, according to the grace given to each of us. If your gift is prophesying, then prophesy in accordance with your faith" (Romans 12:6).

If you cannot release a word and trust God to work it out, do not share it.

Some prophetic words are intended for the encouragement of all who hear them, but not all prophetic words should be delivered in a public setting. There are many words that God intends only for the individuals receiving them to hear. This is especially true when the content of the prophetic word is personal in nature.

There are many things you should not share in a public setting. Some prophetic words may require you to talk privately to the person. If the individual is a child, you may need to discuss the details with his or her parents. God may want you to share with the pastor and let him determine how to best move forward or deliver the word.

God will also show you things that He wants you to discuss with Him alone.

You must learn how to determine the most appropriate method of delivery for the word you receive. The most reliable way to do this is to ask God.

I don't know why, but God tends to do many things like Hansel and Gretel leaving a trail of bread crumbs through the forest. He drops a little bit of information at a time. As you continue to listen, He drops more pieces. Eventually, the bread crumbs lead you to your destination.

God may occasionally give you the whole picture right up front, but that is unusual. He normally gives us little pieces to develop our skills and exercise our faith.

"It is the Spirit of prophecy who bears witness to Jesus" (Revelation 19:10).

All prophetic words are from the mouth of Jesus, about Jesus, for Jesus, to Jesus, and through Jesus. The Father's purpose is to make us look more like His Son. The spirit of prophecy is about what God is doing in your life. He is building Himself inside you every day so you will look more like Him than the day before. Every year you should look back and marvel over how much you have changed. You should be able to say that you are not the same person you were last year. You should identify specific things that have changed because the hand of God was at work in your life.

In prophetic ministry, your words from God are not the equivalent of Scripture, even if they are powerful and anointed by God. Whatever God speaks is eternal for you and will have an effect for the rest of your life. So hold on to it and treasure it like you would a valuable gem, because everything He says to you is precious beyond measure.

He answered and said, "It is written, 'Man shall not live by bread alone, but by every word that proceeds from the mouth of God'" (Matthew 4:4 NKJV).

When the disciples asked Jesus, "Lord, teach us to pray" (Luke 11:1), one of the things that the Bread of Life said was "Give us each day our daily bread" (Luke 11:3). Jesus later explained:

Long ago your people ate the manna in the desert, and they still died. But here is the bread that comes down from heaven. A person can eat it and not die. I am the living bread that came down from heaven. Everyone who eats some of this bread will live forever. This bread is my body. I will give it for the life of the world. (John 6:49–51 NIRV)

Jesus is talking about that continual flow of His word to you, the bread of life that will sustain you forever. You have to live on the bread of His word, which He provides, not what man offers. Eating His provision brings life and truth. It is the perfect nutrition for your spirit to thrive.

John 6 presents an interesting discussion between the disciples and Jesus. Jesus had just performed the miracle of walking on water and was teaching the people, answering their questions, and challenging them to live the life required by God. Then this exchange happened:

Many of His disciples, when they heard this, said, "This is a hard saying; who can understand it?"

When Jesus knew in Himself that His disciples complained about this, He said to them, "Does this offend you? What then if you should see the Son of Man ascend where He was before? It is the Spirit who gives life; the flesh profits nothing. The words that I speak to you are spirit, and they are life. But there are some of you who do not believe." For Jesus knew from the beginning who they were who did not believe, and who would betray Him. And He said, "Therefore I have said to you that no one can come to Me unless it has been granted to him by My Father."

From that time many of His disciples went back and walked with Him no more. Then Jesus said to the twelve, "Do you also want to go away?"

But Simon Peter answered Him, "Lord, to whom shall we go? You have the words of eternal life. Also we have come to believe and know that You are the Christ, the Son of the living God." (John 6:60–69 NKJV)

When challenged by Jesus, the Twelve responded by saying, "We cannot leave. Who else has the words of life? We do not really understand what You are saying, but we recognize the power of God in You and we have nowhere else to go." They recognized that Jesus was the Word. In fact, that is the subject of the whole book of John. Every chapter in that book conveys a different aspect of Jesus. There is a chapter on the water of life, another on the word of life, and the resurrection and the life. John's words point to Jesus and who He became for believers.

With the Word of God always available to you, what else do you need? The continual flow of the Holy Spirit guiding you into what God has for you is also available. God's word lives and moves through you and your life as a testimony not only to you, but also to those around you.

"Not that we are competent in ourselves to claim anything for ourselves, but our competence comes from God. He has made us competent as ministers of a new covenant—not of the letter but of the Spirit; for the letter kills, but the Spirit gives life" (2 Corinthians 3:5–6).

The Bible is the living Word of God and contains the roadmap for all of the issues and situations we face in life. The Bible does not tell us everything we need for the rest of our lives all at once. The Spirit of God speaks to us through the Bible to guide us in making decisions in alignment with God's Word.

The Bible will not tell you whom to marry, what neighborhood to live in, what school to send your kids to, what to name your children, or what career to pursue. But the Holy Spirit can direct you by speaking to you in many ways—through the Word, your dreams, other people, circumstances, signs, and even your own abilities and desires. The key is to always be open to receive what He is speaking to you and remain sensitive to receive it through whatever avenue He chooses. He is always speaking, but are you always listening?

Prophecy is the Spirit's word, and Jesus is the word made flesh.

"The Word became flesh and made his dwelling among us. We have seen his glory, the glory of the one and only Son, who came from the Father, full of grace and truth" (John 1:14).

The spirit of prophecy is Jesus speaking His testimony into your life. It is about Jesus and it is through Jesus. Is the prophetic word you are going to give someone pointing toward Jesus? Is it providing a positive testimony of Him?

Not all prophetic words are created equal, but they are all from God. Some prophecy will change you forever and remain as the North Star of your life, the pillar of your existence. Other prophecies will be things you need to know at a specific moment in time. Both come directly from your Father.

"Above all, you must understand that no prophecy of Scripture came about by the prophet's own interpretation of things. For prophecy never had its origin in the human will, but prophets, though human, spoke from God as they were carried along by the Holy Spirit" (2 Peter 1:20–21).

Prophecy is not an act of human will, but it is a word spoken by God through men moved by the Holy Spirit.

God told Adam and Eve there was only one thing they could not do, and that is exactly what they did. They chose to separate themselves from God. They forfeited that intimate communication when they chose to rebel, and that became typical of human behavior.

God wants to interact with you the same way He did with Adam and Eve in the garden of Eden. Why do you choose a path in life that drives you away from the will of God, away from intimate fellowship with the Creator of the universe rather than closer to it?

God created humanity with the sole intent of fellowship. He longs to restore that intimate fellowship to us today. The Holy

Spirit provides that intimacy for us this side of the cross. My heart's cry is "Forgive me for moving away from that place of intimacy with You, Father. Draw me back to You!" I pray this is your heart's cry as well.

Receiving and delivering prophetic words is wonderful and even fun. However, sometimes an interpretation of the prophetic word is required. While some prophetic words are straightforward and clear, at other times, they require effort to understand.

How do you interpret prophetic words correctly? By studying the Word, praying, and listening to what the Spirit is saying to you. Sometimes understanding will not be given until it is needed.

When Jesus was walking on the beach with Peter and John, He said something to Peter that was neither nice nor kind.

What I'm about to tell you is true. When you were younger, you dressed yourself. You went wherever you wanted to go. But when you are old, you will stretch out your hands. Someone else will dress you. Someone else will lead you where you do not want to go." Jesus said this to point out how Peter would die. His death would bring glory to God. Then Jesus said to him, "Follow me!" (John 21:18–19 NIRV)

As soon as Peter received this word from Jesus, he looked around and saw John. Then Peter asked, "Well, what about that guy, Lord?

Jesus answered, "If I want him to remain alive until I return, what is that to you? You must follow me" (John 21:22).

Peter had just received a prophetic word about his future from Jesus Himself, and he chose to operate from a place of competition and comparison.

Why do we compare ourselves and measure our personal prophetic words from God against another person's experience?

It doesn't matter what God is saying to somebody else or what He plans for others. Grab hold of what He is saying to you. Be thankful for where He is taking you and what He is doing in your life.

A prophecy is a gift from God, an instruction to guide, protect, educate, and bless. He doesn't have to tell us anything, but through His mercy and grace, He talks to us.

Not only is prophecy a gift, it brings gifts. The more you study prophecy, the more blessed you will be. With His guidance, you will walk in the right direction and be in position for many blessings.

> Do not neglect the gift that is in you, which was given to you by prophecy with the laying on of the hands of the eldership. Meditate on these things; give yourself entirely to them, that your progress may be evident to all (1 Timothy 4:14–15 NKJV).

"Look now, I am coming soon! The one who remains true to the prophetic words contained in this book will truly be blessed" (Revelation 22:7 VOICE).

If you focus on your blessing, you will not have time to worry about what is going on with other people.

Jesus wanted Peter to know what God's will was for him. He also let him know that God's will for John was none of his business. This is how we should live also, focused on God's will for our own lives and not in competition or comparison with those around us. We are to work together in unity and do our part to bring about the fulfillment of God's plan for all people to the earth.

The Holy Spirit helps us operate in unity. As we follow God's plan for us and others follow God's plan for them, everyone can operate together as a body, communing with God and reflecting Him to one another. God's original plan was for humankind to work peacefully together as a group. Even though two or three may prophesy, all of us are to judge the word.

Currently, the church is a fellowship of amateurs, not an organization of professionals.

It was God's intention for every believer to be prophetic, to pray for the sick, to cast out devils, and to lead the lost into the kingdom. His plan was never to separate a few select people to do the work of the ministry. It was men who decided that ministry should remain in the hands of a few elite, trained professionals.

Jesus called every believer to fulfill His commission in the earth. While many may be anointed for specific areas of ministry, God does not expect a few people to do each area of ministry alone.

My role is to bring healing to the nations, but I do not pray for every sick person in the world. I teach and train others to do the same work I do.

The body of Christ is equipped through the teachings of the Word, the Holy Spirit, and those whom God has placed in ministry to disciple the nations.

Most prophetic words will require something from you. There are very few prophecies that God fulfills without some action on someone's part. If you do not act on a prophetic word, it usually will not happen, because God is always calling you to Himself and into something deeper.

The best prophetic words are prayed over and have had time to "marinate" in your spirit. While spontaneous words are fun, those that are seasoned in prayer often have more depth and provide more insight into the unseen things of God. It is like the treasure that you spend much time and effort to seek. The more time you spend meditating on what God is saying to you, the more likely it is that you will receive a precise word.

I encourage you to measure the words you receive against some of the things written in this book. As you season them with prayer and fasting, and follow through with the instruction God is giving you, you will see manifestations of the words God is speaking to your heart.

He answered and said to them, "Because it has been given to you to know the mysteries of the kingdom of heaven, but to them it has not been given. For whoever has, to him more will be given, and he will have abundance; but whoever does not have, even what he has will be taken away from him. Therefore I speak to them in parables, because seeing they do not see, and hearing they do not hear, nor do they understand." (Matthew 13:11–13 NKJV)

God's mysteries are available to us when we seek understanding. He will give us even more knowledge and insight as we study His Word. Many hear or see what is happening today and do not understand the spiritual meaning of world events or words being spoken.

In Matthew 7:7 and Luke 11:9, Jesus said, "Seek and you will find." That certainly applies to wisdom about prophecy.

First Corinthians 14:5 (TLB) says, "I wish you all had the gift of 'speaking in tongues,' but even more I wish you were all able to prophesy, preaching God's messages, for that is a greater and more useful power than to speak in unknown languages."

The Names of God Bible says, "I wish that all of you could speak in other languages, but especially that you could speak what God has revealed. The person who speaks what God has revealed is more important than the person who speaks in other languages."

Prophecy is more important than tongues when it comes to ministering to other people. Only God can understand speaking or praying in tongues unless there is an interpreter. When you prophesy, you are speaking in a known language and can explain directly to the person receiving the word from God.

CHAPTER 10

Real-Life Examples of Prophetic Words

To this point, we have talked about the prophetic word and how it operates. Now I'd like to share with you some examples of prophecy and its manifestation in people's lives.

WITTY INVENTIONS

I recently received a text message from someone I prophesied over in May 2012. He and his wife were associate pastors of a church at the time. The Lord gave me a prophetic word for them, and I told them, "God is getting ready to open up the windows of heaven. He will give you an amazing, witty invention. Things you have dreamed about and wanted to have, you will get. He will open a door for it to happen."

The pastor recorded what I said on his phone and he listened to it every week, praying, "Okay, God, I am standing on this word, but I have no clue what Joan was talking about."

Six or seven months later, he received an idea and acted on what God gave him. In his recent text, he said, "We are launching it." This invention will help people around the world. And bring in millions of dollars for him.

When we get a prophetic word, we want to see it manifested immediately. Usually, we need to wait and continue seeking God for the answer or its manifestation. This pastor did not just receive the word, place it on a shelf, and say, "If God wants it to come to pass, it will." Instead, he sought God and listened to the prophetic word over and over again to get it deep within his spirit. God gave him the idea, but he had to follow through to activate the prophecy. If he had just said, "Oh that's a cool idea," and never did anything about it, it would not have happened.

Recommitment and Restoration

I was shopping with a couple of members of our ministry team one day. While the cashier checked us out, and I was chatting casually with her, God dropped a word for her into my spirit.

I said, "I have a word for you. God really misses you. He misses you at church and He misses talking with you. Would it be okay if I led you in a prayer to recommit your life to God?"

"You're freaking me out," she said. She told me what denomination she was affiliated with, which explained her reaction.

"That's okay," I said. "But when you go home tonight and get ready for bed, I'd like you to say this prayer."

I gave her a brief prayer of recommitment, and she repeated

the prayer with me. I left hoping she would pray it again that night. If she did, I knew it would turn out to be a major step that would alter her life significantly from that moment on.

If you are willing to hear God and then take the step of faith to deliver His message to another person, it will happen. Doing so can seem scary if you don't know the person God has called you to deliver a message to. Speaking a prophetic word to a stranger requires a certain level of faith. I encourage you to be sensitive to the Holy Spirit and speak. Your obedience could be the very thing that restores someone to a right relationship with God and saves his or her soul.

ACCEPTING THE CALL OF GOD

Prophesying is not just about delivering a word to someone in church. In fact, a great number of prophetic words I give to people are outside the church setting—in public situations and many times to strangers.

I was on a plane one day when God gave me a word for the flight attendant. As I started to get up, the plane hit a little turbulence, so I sat back down. I knew God wanted me to deliver that word. Even though I could not do it right away, I determined to give it to him one way or another. When it was time to get off the plane, I left with the other passengers but waited in the Jetway while he finished cleaning. When he got off the plane, I said to him, "Hi. I have a word for you from the Lord."

"Okay," he said, looking a bit skeptical.

"You are walking the wrong aisles, serving coffee and tea. God wants you to serve His Word and feed His people."

He raised an eyebrow. "You and my mother."

I chuckled. "God has been trying to speak to you through

your mom, but you haven't listened. So God picked a stranger on this plane to speak to you."

He nodded. "I know you're right. I need to do what God has called me to do."

Sometimes people need a little kick to get them out of their comfort zone and into all that God has for them. If you want to be used by God, you have to be willing to speak no matter where you are.

Prophesying is simply a matter of listening to the Holy Spirit and knowing that God orders your steps. He will place you in the perfect place at the perfect time. Where are you right now? Do you know why you are there? Ask God to show you, listen, and deliver the word He gives you to the person He chooses. It could mean the difference between eternity with God or without Him.

PROPHESYING THE SCRIPTURES

I learned how to prophesy by the examples I read in Scripture and by observing others who move in the prophetic. At our ministry events, we use a brochure called "the blue sheet." It is filled with Scriptures to declare, decree, and prophesy into your future as well as to claim when you give financial offerings to God.

For instance, some people give $111 a week based on Deuteronomy 1:11: "May the Lord, the God of your ancestors, increase you a thousand times and bless you as He has promised!"

Prophetically, this means that the Lord God of your fathers will make you a thousand times more numerous than you are and bless you as He has promised. This takes a promise from the

Scripture and makes it into a word for today because you need to work on your "now."

I teach people in all of my conferences, miracles services, and healing schools to find a Scripture, sow a seed for that Scripture, and prophesy the Word of God over their lives as they give. When you do this, God will respond to your faith in His Word.

I do not want to wait years to be blessed a thousand times more than I am. I want to receive all the blessings that God has for me *now*.

"My God will meet all your needs according to the riches of his glory in Christ Jesus" (Philippians 4:19). My God will supply all of my needs according to His riches in glory—today, right now!

"Take delight in the Lord, and he will give you the desires of your heart" (Psalm 37:4). As I take delight in the Lord, He will give me the desires of my heart.

These are just a few examples of how you can take the Scriptures, personalize them, and create declarations and decrees over your life. Speak these Scriptures aloud daily and watch what God does for you!

God has given me many Scriptures that I have made personal. John 3:16 is one of my favorites: "For God so loved *Joan* that He gave His only begotten Son, that if *Joan* believes in Him *she* should not perish but have everlasting life" (John 3:16 NKJV). Insert your name in place of mine and read that aloud. It is awesome when you get a personal revelation of the Word, seeing and hearing your name woven into the Scriptures.

Another Scripture I like to read in my services is Ephesians 1:17–19, which says:

I keep asking that the God of our Lord Jesus Christ, the glorious Father, may give you the Spirit of wisdom and revelation, so that you may know him better. I pray that the eyes of your heart may be enlightened in order that you may know the hope to which he has called you, the riches of his glorious inheritance in his holy people, and his incomparably great power for us who believe.

When I read this passage prophetically in services, or when I decree it over someone, it sounds something like this:

Today, the God of our Lord Jesus Christ, the Father of glory, is giving you a greater spirit of revelation and wisdom and a greater knowledge of Him. The eyes of your understanding are being opened so you will know what He has called you to do. You will experience the riches of the glory of His inheritance in the saints. You will also experience the exceeding greatness of His power toward you because you believe according to the working of His mighty power.

God wants to anoint the Word and make it prophetic and personal for you. Start confessing Isaiah 49:25 aloud: "Yes, captives will be taken from warriors, and plunder retrieved from the fierce; I will contend with those who contend with you."

That passage in itself is awesome. But then it continues with "and I will save your children" (NLT). Once you start prophesying those words over yourself and your family, you will see incredible breakthroughs in your family's lives, bringing them to salvation and also blessing them greatly.

UNDERSTANDING THE PROPHETIC THROUGH NATURAL CIRCUMSTANCES

Many times, God tries to speak to us through natural events. When a situation happens in the world, I ask, "God, are You trying to tell me something through this particular situation?"

For example, a few years ago, some meteors came crashing into our atmosphere. One of them hit the earth approximately seventeen thousand miles away, in Russia. I fly more than seventeen thousand miles a month on an airplane, and we had ministered in Russia recently, so this event felt almost personal.

I asked God what He wanted to reveal through this meteor. God replied, "Here I am. I am coming. My blessings have been released from the heavenlies, poured out to bless you." Then He added, "This is a sign that My healing power will hit Russia like they have never known before. Russia will have a revival like they have never seen before."

The next time I was in Russia, I delivered that prophetic word. This ministry brought revival, because the healing power of God hit Russia in an incredible way. Our team will soon go back to do a healing school and teach the Russian people how to minister healing, so their nation can be healed and brought into a deeper relationship with Jesus.

When unusual things happen in the natural realm, ask, "God, are You trying to speak to me through this?" For instance, if you were to encounter some roadblocks while you were driving to your intended destination, you may think, *I won't get there on time because of all these delays.* Look beyond the natural situation and ask God what He is trying to say to you. Maybe you are walking ahead of His plan. An accident could be waiting up ahead. If you arrive to your destination too early, you may miss someone He wants you to touch.

What kind of delays or obstacles are you experiencing in your personal life? In order to move forward into all God has for you, get rid of any unnecessary congestion in your life.

Some delays may be from God, but not all.

James Goll, a friend of mine, came to our ministry headquarters in Texas to minister several years ago. One day, as he was preaching, he looked at me and said, "God has called you to the French."

I immediately thought, *Yes! I'm going to Paris! Eiffel Tower, here I come! I can already taste the delicious crepes and pommes frites. Hallelujah!*

Not wanting to jump to a conclusion and assume I knew what God meant, I asked Him for clarification and confirmation. "God, have You really called me to Paris? Or maybe Canada? Or somewhere else?"

About a month later, I got a phone call. "An earthquake has hit Haiti. While we were discussing a solution, the only name that came up was Hunter. So we are calling to see if you will go to Haiti and bring healing to that devastated nation."

I answered yes, even though in my mind I was screaming, *No!* I dreaded the thought of spending nights on rocks in a sleeping bag. Fortunately, God provided a mission house and we did not have to rough it quite as much as I feared.

We can easily interpret a prophetic word our way instead of God's way. I had initially interpreted the prophetic word from James Goll to mean that God had called me to minister to people in Paris. I'd always thought the Haitians were Spanish. But I learned that they are French Creole.

Sometimes God has bigger plans for us than we think or

want. His plan for me was bigger than going to Paris. It was such a blessing to be part of God's work and to witness how He can heal hearts and transform lives in a country devastated by a natural disaster.

After obedience to His direction, I visited Paris and brought God's healing to the country of France as well. I even have pictures of myself standing in front of the Eiffel Tower. God gave me the desire of my heart because I was willing to put His kingdom first by taking His healing power to the French in Haiti. I got the best of both worlds.

Following God to Haiti led to incredible doors of opportunity for continued ministry and outreach in that country. We have been able to continue our mission work there over the years and now have an amazing outreach there. I function as an apostle over Haiti and the people there call me the "mother of Haiti."

God did call me to the French—just not the people I expected.

I could have forced God's hand and gone to Paris after James Goll gave that word to me. If I had forced the timing and meaning of the prophetic word to be France, and scheduled a ministry event there outside of God's timing, it would have gone nowhere.

One day in late 2012, Doug Addison received some prophetic words. He logged them into a journal on January 1, then sent them out electronically on January 2. His words were so right on, I thought Doug was prophesying directly to me and that he knew my circumstances.

On February 3, Doug prophesied that God would speak to the world through a natural event. His Daily Prophetic Word that day said, "A prophetic sign from God will be seen around the world."

Greatly anticipating what this word would be, I couldn't wait to see what God was going to do.

That Sunday was the Super Bowl game between the Ravens and the Forty-Niners at Candlestick Park. Before the game, Doug walked around the field, saying, "God will speak to the world through Candlestick Park."

If you're a football fan, you may remember that the electrical power went out during the third quarter. The score was 28 to 6. Adding those numbers together makes thirty-four. The power was out for thirty-four minutes. The power outage happened in the third quarter (3/4). At the end of the game, the winning team's score was 34. Three and four equals seven. We considered that these numbers may have prophetic significance.

As Doug sought God for added understanding of this event, the Holy Spirit led him to Ezekiel 34, which talks about the lack of love God's people showed to those who had been wounded or hurt—spiritual outcasts. Doug wrote an in-depth discussion about this and put it on his website.[2]

Biblically, ravens represent provision. And the Ravens won over the Forty-Niners, a term used in 1849 for people who went to California for the gold rush. Prophetically, according to Doug, that Super Bowl game meant that from that point onward there was going to be a time of breakthrough for provision and finances.

Another part of that prophetic word was that most Christians are not operating at full power. God has so much more power to offer, but His children do not know how to activate it. Prophesying is about releasing the power of the Holy Spirit within us.

---

2 http://dougaddison.com/2016/02/did-you-see-these-prophetic-signs-in-the-super-bowl/.

When things happen in the natural realm, you might get a prophetic word related to them. So pay attention to natural events and ask God for the spiritual significance. God is continually speaking. We just have to be willing to listen and pray about the signs He is giving us through the circumstances around us.

CHAPTER 11

The Timing of Prophetic Words

It is always important to know when to give a prophetic word. Sometimes I will have a word and know who the word is for. The word may apply to other people as well, and I always hope they will receive the word too.

If you hear a prophetic word that God gives to someone else and you believe it is for you also, you can receive it. Even though it was spoken over somebody else, you can say, "I receive that word too." The prophet's finger does not have to point at you for you to receive. Listen to the words given to other people, and if they could apply to your life, just say, "I will take that one and that one and that one."

I am quick to claim almost all of the prophetic words that I hear. Of course, if the word is "You're going to have a baby," I would not want that one. Grandchildren, yes. New souls into the kingdom, definitely. New ministries birthed, absolutely. However, no more physical babies for me!

About twenty-five years ago, I prophesied over a couple who had just gotten married, saying, "God will give you a son." They were excited and praised God for this great news. She became pregnant and gave birth to a precious baby girl. She became pregnant again and had another girl. A few years later, she had a third daughter. Was the prophetic word wrong?

Fast forward several years. When one of their daughters had graduated from college, my friend went to the doctor because she didn't feel well. the doctor told her she was pregnant.

"No, I'm not," she said. "I'm forty-seven years old!"

Almost a year later, she sent me a picture of her new baby with a note that said, "Guess what? Your prophetic word was right on. I now have the son you prophesied about more than twenty years ago."

When you prophesy something like having a child, it may not happen right away. But if God said it, it will happen—in His time.

Maybe you receive a prophetic word that says, "I see you around lots of children." And you think, *That is awesome!* You love children and you are excited about all the kids you are going to have. But God might be calling you to work with children, not necessarily give birth to them.

Ask God to develop your ear in the area of the prophetic. When you receive a word, seek His heart and His interpretation on the word. Don't assume you know what it means.

When a prophecy is from God, He will work out the details and open the doors.

God may give you a prophetic word for someone, but He

might intend it be delivered later. Occasionally, God has given me prophetic words for the end of a service, at the beginning of another service, or even days ahead of time. God knows when the person receiving the word needs to hear it, so don't get over-excited when you receive something from God. Wait to deliver it when God says the time is right.

When you prophesy over somebody, God may show you what they are experiencing or feeling as they receive His message. Some people call it "reading your mail" because it is so personal and specifically directed to them. It's exciting to share a personal word of encouragement with someone. But no matter how specific the word, it is important that you give it in His timing.

Understanding the Purpose of Trials

When you are going through trials or difficult times, you may believe you have done something wrong or acted in disobedience. While that can be the case, more frequently it is not about anything you have done. It is more often something you are experiencing that will give you a personal status update (or report card) on where you are spiritually and to push you deeper in your walk with Jesus. It can also help you mature and grow in greater wisdom in Christ. James puts it this way:

> Consider it pure joy, my brothers and sisters, whenever you face trials of many kinds, because you know that the testing of your faith produces perseverance. Let perseverance finish its work so that you may be mature and complete, not lacking anything. (James 1:2–4)

Do not listen to individuals who tell you that every test or trial is the result of sin. If you are going through a difficult season, that does not mean you are in disobedience. Instead, consider it an opportunity to examine yourself and your actions. Facing a hard time at work or in your family does not mean that you are in the wrong place at the wrong time. Instead of trying to get out of the difficult situation, ask yourself these questions:

- Why is this attack happening?

- What is the purpose behind it?

- Am I in disobedience?

- Am I missing a key obedience factor here?

- How can I learn and grow from this?

- What is the wisdom of God that can see me through?

As you ponder these questions and bring things into alignment, stretch your faith muscles and know that God will see you through. There is always victory and a good testimony on the other side of a trial.

When I pray for people who are going through a difficult time, I ask God to give me a word of encouragement that will speak to their specific situation and touch them right where they are. God often gives me a word to give them the strength they need to keep pressing forward into their breakthrough.

God usually speaks clearly, but sometimes in unique and unexpected ways.

For example, my daughter Melody once asked God to give her a word of encouragement for a friend she was praying for.

God did not drop a magical envelope down from heaven with a letter inside. Instead, He chose to speak to her through the information printed on the back label of a shampoo bottle!

When she looked at the many chemical ingredients on the label, she saw one that looked similar to the word *psalm*. Then she saw the numbers 3, 7, 10, and 13. Hoping they were some of the nicer Psalms, she opened her Bible and looked them up.

Psalm 3 was about David going through a trial. Psalm 7 was about David going through another trial. Psalm 10 was also about David going through a trial. She asked the Lord what this meant. In Psalm 13, she found the final key to the message.

In that psalm, David expressed his thankfulness for how God had turned everything around. Then it all made perfect sense. God wanted Melody's friends to know that after their trials were over, He would bring a season of healing in their lives.

This family had been going through one trial after another. They didn't understand why they were experiencing so many struggles if they were in His will. They had been praying, "God, is this where You have called us to be? If not, what are You calling us to do?"

God's answer was "Yes, this is where I have called you. I want you to continue to persevere through all these trials. Then you will fully realize that this is My place for you." The word God gave Melody to pass on to them confirmed that they were on the right path and that the hand of God would bring them what they needed.

If God can use words and numbers on a shampoo bottle to get a message to you, He can use anything. Be open to receive God's message and follow the clues that He leaves for you.

What is He using to speak to you today? Pay attention to the Holy Spirit and the impressions He births in your spirit. Then be bold enough to step out in faith, deliver the word, and trust God to minister to the hearts of the people who listen.

Not long ago, my friends Cindy and Spencer from Nordyke Ministries were at a coffee shop, working on a computer. A college-age girl sat next to them, wearing a headset and apparently doing her homework. Another girl walked over to her, said, "Hi," and began talking to her. When she said, "What's Mom making for dinner tonight?" Cindy realized the girls were sisters.

The college-age girl started answering, "Mom's making chicken—" but then she stopped and asked, "Are you wearing my shirt?"

The girl replied, "I don't know, is it yours? It was in my closet."

"Oh. Well, if it was in your closet, I guess it's okay."

When Cindy heard that, the Holy Ghost said, "Cindy, what is in your closet? Salvation is in your closet. Healing is in your closet. Finances are in your closet. Abundance is in your closet." The Lord directed her to Matthew 6:6, which says, "When you pray, go into your room, close the door and pray to your Father, who is unseen. Then your Father, who sees what is done in secret, will reward you."

God also told Cindy, "What you are wearing is okay, even if it belongs to someone else."

God used a natural circumstance and the conversation of people around Cindy to speak a prophetic word of encouragement to her heart. Because she was sensitive enough to pay attention to what was happening and to hear the spiritual application of it, God was able to speak to her. He used this event to deliver a message for her own life and for those she shares it with—including you as you read this book! Now you too can receive that word for your life.

God has given you things that are hanging in your closet. If He has placed something in there, you can wear it.

Examine things in the natural and ask, "God, are You trying to teach me something through this?"

CHAPTER 12

Prophetic Application of Scripture

God's Word is always available to help you through difficult times and seasons. He can give you prophetic words through others, but He also gives you specific Scriptures to lean on during certain chapters of your life. For example, if your hopes and dreams seem destroyed and you are struggling to trust God for good things in your future, God may give you Jeremiah 29:11 to stand on: "'I know the plans I have for you,' declares the Lord, 'plans to prosper you and not to harm you, plans to give you hope and a future.'"

This Scripture is very meaningful to me. There have been times when my family has gone through such difficult experiences that all we had was Scripture to stand on. When you have Scriptures to see you through hard times, disasters and crises can work on your behalf for your ultimate good. How? They teach you to stretch your faith and deepen your walk with God.

My daughter Melody was eighteen years old when her father and I divorced. She was involved in a great church with a wonderful community of believers her age to support her during that time. However, because of everything our family went through, she was emotionally on edge and could not stop crying. In the midst of this difficult time, she described herself as feeling like a "basket case." She did not understand why her dad, who was also her pastor, could be unfaithful to me, her mom. She felt as if the entire foundation of her life was completely gone. The situation devastated her world.

Today, I can look back and see God's timing. Shortly before the divorce, Melody got a job at the Galleria in Dallas. It was a small shop with only one person working there at a time, except during the Christmas season, when there were two.

Her boss told her she could do whatever she wanted when the store was empty. "You can talk to your friends on the phone or do homework if you want. But if somebody walks in the door, you will immediately stop whatever you're doing and take care of them."

When business was slow, she did her homework and read her Bible, encouraging herself with the Word of God. She spent a lot of time studying the Psalms. As she went through the Word, she copied into her journal any Scriptures that stood out for that day.

Melody was very fragile emotionally and didn't believe she would make it because the things she had trusted in were gone. Her entire reality had shifted. But Scripture saw her through that difficult and challenging time in her life. God was faithful!

I asked Melody to share some of those Scriptures in this

book. These core verses have carried her from that crisis at eighteen until the present day. She has consistently claimed these Scriptures for her life and prophesied them over herself. As you read them, I pray that you too will find strength from them. If they speak to your life situation right now, prophesy them over yourself and watch what God will do for you.

BEING THANKFUL IN HARD TIMES

"I will praise You, O Lord, with my whole heart; I will tell of all Your marvelous works. I will be glad and rejoice in You; I will sing praise to Your name, O Most High" (Psalm 9:1–2 NKJV).

Speak that verse over yourself right now. Say, "God, today I will give thanks to You with my whole heart. I will tell anyone and everyone how wonderful You are. No matter what, I will be glad and rejoice in all that You have done for me. I will continue to sing praises to Your name."

By making the Word personal, you breathe its life into your spirit. "Today, God, I am going to work. I will have a good attitude when I deal with my boss. I will be thankful for the job I have and do it to the best of my ability. I am going to be faithful, God. When people ask me about You, I will tell them how You provided a wonderful job for me. I will be glad and rejoice in You. Thank You for giving me something to rejoice about and be thankful for."

Never forget all that God has done for you. You can get through hard times when you focus on the good things you have received and that you enjoy. Make those the center of your daily meditation. Write down all the ways God has blessed you. Repeat them aloud whenever you feel down or depressed. Thank Him for every item on your list.

Rejoice in God's Faithfulness

"I've thrown myself headlong into your arms—I'm celebrating your rescue. I'm singing at the top of my lungs, I'm so full of answered prayers" (Psalm 13:5–6 MSG).

Remember times in the past when God was good and faithful to you or your family. Since He has brought you through dark waters repeatedly, why wouldn't He to do it again in your current circumstances? Never forget His many benefits or what He has done for you. Make this declaration: "God, today I am going to trust in Your unfailing love and rejoice in my salvation. This situation is temporary. Your best for my life is coming. It is right around the corner and I rejoice in victory right now!"

When a person who needs to hear from God doesn't know what she is supposed to do with her life or is facing depression, I pray: "God, remind her to rejoice in her salvation." If you cannot find anything else to be thankful for, thank Him for your salvation. Thank Him for being a gracious and loving God and for sending a Savior to set you free. No matter how things look, come back to the cross and say, "Thank You!" This alone can change your life.

God Is Your Rock

"The Lord is my rock, my fortress and my deliverer; my God is my rock, in whom I take refuge, my shield and the horn of my salvation, my stronghold" (Psalm 18:2).

A fortress is a heavily protected structure. Imagine a castle, with a moat filled with water that goes all the way around it.

Now imagine that God created you as a castle. He is the water surrounding you so your enemies cannot overtake you.

He has established you in a safe and secure position under His protection.

Repeat this verse as your verbal declaration: "The Lord is my rock, my fortress, and my savior; my God is my rock, in whom I find protection. He is my shield, the power that saves me, and my place of safety" (Psalm 18:2 NLT).

There is no better piece of armor available than God as your shield, standing between you and the darts of the enemy: sickness or disease. He is standing between you and total destruction. Trust Him to be the one who unconditionally stands as your protection and stronghold.

GOD RESCUES YOU FROM TROUBLE

"But me he caught—reached all the way from sky to sea; he pulled me out of that ocean of hate, that enemy chaos, the void in which I was drowning. They hit me when I was down, but God stuck by me. He stood me up on a wide-open field; I stood there saved—surprised to be loved!" (Psalm 18:16–19 MSG).

The worship song "Oceans" is one of my favorites. When I sing the chorus, I feel as if I am crying out for salvation. When it talks about resting in God's embrace and belonging to Him, I cannot help but picture a husband and wife. The safest place a wife could be is in the arms of her husband.

This is the picture God gives His bride as He says, "Let Me embrace you. Let Me engulf you. Let Me be your protector. Allow Me be your shield. This is how safe you are." Acknowledge the safety and protection He brings to your life.

During 2013–2014, that song was a prophetic calling for the ministry team to trust and say, "God, wherever You are calling us, wherever You are leading us, we will go. We know that You will keep our eyes above the water. When we cannot control the circumstances, Your hand is moving. Our souls will find rest in You."

Matthew 14 tells the story about Peter walking on the water. I don't know if God will ever call me to physically walk on water, but I believe that He knows the storms I face in life and listens when I cry, "God, keep my eyes above the water."

This does not mean the waters will never rise or that there won't be any storms. God is not saying that you will be on top of the raging waters the whole time. But He does call you to move to that secret place where your soul will find rest. The most secure place for you to find peace is in the arms of God.

Declare Psalm 18:17–19 by saying, "God, I thank You for reaching down to where I am standing and putting Your hand on things that I cannot conquer, for shutting the mouths of my enemies and those who would stand against me. God, thank You for loving me. Let my life be a delight to You."

When you make Scripture personal, you can own what God says to you. Pray, "God, thank You for taking me out of this pit of depression, out of the watery grave I'm in. Thank You for saving me and not leaving me here alone."

You can find a lot of encouragement in the book of Psalms. Even one Psalm can encourage you in many areas of your life.

GOD'S WAYS ARE PERFECT

"I don't think the way you think. The way you work isn't the way I work. ... For as the sky soars high above earth, so the way I work surpasses the way you work, and the way I think is beyond the way you think. Just as rain and snow descend from the skies and don't go back until they've watered the earth, doing their work of making things grow and blossom, producing seed for farmers and food for the hungry, so will the words that come out of my mouth not come back empty-handed. They'll do the work I sent them to do, they'll complete the assignment I gave them" (Isaiah 55:8–9 MSG).

"As for God, his way is perfect: the Lord's word is flawless; he shields all who take refuge in him. For who is God besides the Lord? And who is the Rock except our God? It is God who arms me with strength and keeps my way secure. He makes my feet like the feet of a deer; he causes me to stand on the heights" (Psalm 18:30–33).

You can prophesy over your own life by saying, "God, I thank You that Your thoughts are not my thoughts and Your ways are better than my ways. Your way is perfect. No matter what I am planning, You will show me your perfect plan that gives me hope and a good future."

"'No weapon formed against you shall prosper, and every tongue which rises against you in judgment you shall condemn. This is the heritage of the servants of the Lord, and their righteousness is from Me,' says the Lord" (Isaiah 54:17 NKJV).

If you are wrongfully involved in a court case, read Isaiah 54:17 from The Living Bible: "In that coming day, no weapon turned against you shall succeed, and you will have justice against every courtroom lie. This is the heritage of the servants of the Lord. This is the blessing I have given you, says the Lord."

These verses should be every Christian's anthem. Prophesy that verse to yourself.

In no way will any weapon formed against me prosper, because God will not let the enemy beat me down. Even if I have a momentary weakness or setback, I will declare, "God, thank You for making my way perfect and leading

me to the path that You have for my life. Thank You,
Father, that You will fight my battles for me."

Guard Your Words

"May these words of my mouth and this meditation of my heart
be pleasing in your sight, Lord, my Rock and my Redeemer"
(Psalm 19:14).

You can declare and prophesy over yourself every day by saying, "God, guard every word that comes out of my mouth today.
Delight in my words and let the words of my mouth and the
thoughts of my heart please You."

My parents were married for thirty-nine years. It seems like
a record now, since many marriages these days only last a few
years. One day my mom was trying to explain to me why she
and my father had a successful marriage. She said, "When you
get married, be honest with your husband, even to the piece of a
thought."

I asked, "How do you share 'to the piece of a thought'?"

She said, "Share everything with him and withhold nothing
from him." She knew the enemy could attack a marriage through
the couple's thoughts. He will come in wherever he can find an
open door. If he can cause division between your thoughts and
the Word, or between you and your spouse, he will use that to
gain entry to destroy you.

Do not give a place to word plays, thoughts, or suggestions
you know you should not trust. If you allow this, the little foxes
will spoil the grapes (see Song of Solomon 2:15). When circumstances come against you, the more of the Word you obey, the
longer you will be able to stand.

When you are waiting for a doctor's confirmation on

something—even if the issue is not serious—the enemy will attack your mind with fearful thoughts. Every time the enemy sends negative thoughts your way, declare, "This is not true. It is a lie, because I know that God is my healer, my fortress, and my shield. He is my Savior." Prophesy truth over your situation.

Just as my mom and dad had a marriage based on honesty, God wants us to be honest with Him in every thought. When negative thoughts that are not of God creep in, you can be honest and say, "This is where I'm struggling, God. I am taking every thought captive and renouncing fear. Even in a worst-case scenario, I will praise You. I will glorify You and say to the devil, 'All this worry you tried to give me—I will not receive it. Take it back and leave now!'"

GOD GIVES YOU DIRECTION

"Show me your ways, Lord, teach me your paths. Guide me in your truth and teach me, for you are God my Savior, and my hope is in you all day long" (Psalm 25:4–5).

When you lack clear direction in your life, hang on to this Scripture. Declare, "God, I have no idea what I am doing in my life, but I trust You to lead me. Give me a clue, an insight, a hint. Show me Your ways, Lord, so that I can walk in them."

God has a future and a hope for you. Yet many times we say, "God, give me a clue. What are You doing in my life? Please whisper in my ear and give me direction."

I understand the frustrations that can come from not knowing exactly what God wants you to do. There have been many transitional periods in my life when I wondered what God was doing and where He was taking me. Through all of those times of uncertainty, I could always say, "God, through Your Scriptures, show me and guide me. Make my paths straight (Proverbs 3:6). Make my feet like hinds' feet (Psalm 18:33). Thank You for ordaining my steps."

GOD TURNS YOUR SORROW TO JOY

"You turned my wailing into dancing; you removed my sackcloth and clothed me with joy, that my heart may sing your praises and not be silent. Lord my God, I will praise you forever" (Psalm 30:11–12).

No matter what difficulties you face, no matter what grief has tried to overtake you, in the midst of pain you can still declare, "God, I thank You that today is the last day of my sorrow. God, thank You that my sorrow will be gone in the newness of the morning. Thank You for clothing me with joy!" Declare and decree this over your life every day until you receive your breakthrough. God will shift your condition if you trust Him and rely on Him to do it.

There is a difference between joy and happiness. Happiness is an emotion you feel based on temporary circumstances. Joy is something that is born in your spirit and has nothing to do with your present situation. You can say, "God, let joy overflow." When you allow joy to flow, it will overtake your situation. The joy in your spirit will change the sorrow in your heart to fulfillment—independent from your surroundings.

"The Lord is close to the brokenhearted and saves those who are crushed in spirit" (Psalm 34:18).

This verse describes a season of my life when I was emotionally crying out to God. I identified with David. I felt distraught, let down, disappointed, and brokenhearted. Now I can look back and say, "This verse is how I made it through and avoided a nervous breakdown."

Painful situations happen in life. Emotions seem to overtake you and you may feel like a wreck. You are a very important person, created in the image of God with a vast array of emotions. God gave you these emotions to help you filter and cleanse yourself from the stress, trauma, and heartbreak of life. It's okay to cry. When tears come, they help you release painful emotions. It is not healthy to ignore them, push them down, or internalize them.

God made us emotional beings. There are times when we are faced with problems we don't want to deal with. We try to avoid them by keeping ourselves occupied so we do not think about them. We ignore the problem until it becomes something we can no longer control. We may put off dealing with it for so long that we believe there is no need to worry about it because it is over. That behavior might work for a while, but eventually, the emotions will surface.

It is best to confront how you feel and let God minister to you in the midst of your pain rather than running from it. Embrace the pain and allow God to heal you. It may hurt for a season, but in time, you will experience a greater level of wholeness and well-being.

Find Scriptures that apply to your situation and declare them daily. Allow the Word to wash over you and cleanse the negative, the sadness, the pain from your body and mind. Your words will be a positive prophecy to heal and restore you physically, emotionally, and spiritually.

My daughter once took a personality test. It asked questions like "If you could do this or that, which one would you choose?" The purpose of the test was to reveal the areas of her interest or qualities she needed to develop in her character. The results indicated she was emotional.

Her first thought was *Of course! I'm a girl. And I don't care if you say I am emotional.* Then she decided to analyze the results of the test and allow God to flow through her. *God,* she prayed, *help me with my anger. Show me my unmet or unrealistic expectations. Show me how to love in a greater way, and give me better control over my emotions.*

God revealed truths to her and showed her the parts of her personality that He gave her to lead and be creative. She is very gifted and a tremendous blessing to me, the ministry, and the kingdom of God. When she recognized her gifts and embraced what God had given her, she was able to grow and develop in those areas.

Instead of trying to ignore emotions and avoid doing anything about them, pray, "God, help me develop in this area. Help me to use the gifts You have placed inside me and turn them into a vehicle to help people and glorify Your name."

Learn to Control Your Emotions

"My dear brothers and sisters, take note of this: Everyone should be quick to listen, slow to speak and slow to become angry" (James 1:19).

This is a great Scripture to declare and prophesy over yourself if you struggle with anger, frustration, or stress when you deal with people. Thank God that He has given you the Holy Spirit. Pray, "God, help me to be slow to speak, quick to listen, and slow to anger. Help me eliminate any unrealistic expectations I have for the people around me. Help me see them through Your eyes, God. Keep me from speaking in anger or frustration."

Uncontrolled emotions can be trapped in your body and cause an illness or disease. Unresolved anger can cause a multitude of health and relational issues in your life. Eventually emotions surface in one way or another.

It is okay to be angry as long as you express your anger in a godly way, without sin. Holding on to anger or lashing out at others is not acceptable to God. When you are angry, do not allow your emotions to lead you into sin or cause you to harm another person.

What do emotions and prophecy have to do with each other? Prophecy has to be delivered carefully. You do not know whether the words you deliver will be well received or not. You open your mouth and speak the words God gives you for people. Since some words are positive and happy, you may join them in rejoicing. However, God may be giving a serious word that may require your compassion and strict emotional control.

A word of prophecy should not be given roughly or to cause pain. Control your emotions, your tone of voice, and your manner of dealing with the person(s) receiving the prophecy. Speak with God's voice, compassion, and love.

Help Those Around You Who Are in Need

"Carry each other's burdens, and in this way you will fulfill the law of Christ" (Galatians 6:2).

Part of living a successful Christian life and flowing in the prophetic is being sensitive to the needs of those around you. When you ask God to empower you to minister to your brothers and sisters in Christ, He will position you to move in the prophetic flow of the Holy Spirit. He may speak to you about a specific thing you could do to help someone, or He may give you a word of encouragement to help him along his way. Make this your declaration: "God, help me to fulfill the law of Jesus Christ by loving others like You do. God, give me compassion for those in need. Open my eyes to those around me who need You."

Speak to the Mountains

"Truly I tell you, if anyone says to this mountain, 'Go, throw yourself into the sea,' and does not doubt in their heart but believes that what they say will happen, it will be done for them" (Mark 11:23).

At one time, we were ministering in New Jersey and teaching on the prophetic. My daughter was with me on this trip and she was asking God to give her a word for the meetings. She kept praying over and over, "God, give me a word."

During the service, she prayed more specifically. "God, give me a word for those who are coming to the meeting tomorrow."

The Lord said, "Tell the ladies."

"Tell them what?" she asked.

Again God said, "Tell the ladies."

Again she asked, "Tell them what? There has to be something more to this."

When she got up to share the next day, she said, "God has revealed that we are all called to face different mountains. He wants you to speak to your own particular mountain, for it to be removed."

In this service, the audience was all women except for one man. Since God had told her to "Tell the ladies," Melody was surprised that a man was there, but his presence did not make her prophetic word any less true. All those who were facing difficulty needed to know they could speak to and remove their mountains.

As you prophesy over yourself, speak to those mountains in

your life, the strongholds from which God wants to set you free. Pray, "God, remove these things that are not of You. Make my paths straight according to Your Word so I can walk in the freedom of obedience."

God sometimes gives my husband, Kelley, prophetic words weeks in advance of a meeting. At one conference, God gave him several words for those who would be attending three weeks before the meeting. Each time he shared during the conference, I thought, *Oh, that's a really cool word.*

Kelley kept giving words for people by name. It shows real trust in the Lord when we call out, "Is so-and-so here?" because we don't know who will be in the services.

Toward the end of the meeting, Kelley said, "This word is for Suzanne."

No one raised a hand.

Kelley asked, "Is there a Suzanne here?"

Melody's middle name is Suzanne, but Kelley did not know this word was for her. Otherwise, he would have said, "Joan, God gave me a word for Melody." Instead, God did it with stealth, giving Kelley this word three weeks before the service, especially for her, without using her first name.

God will give you specific words for specific purposes at just the right place and time.

Use Scriptures to speak life over yourself and others. Let God show you how to develop an ear to hear His voice and a heart of compassion to respond appropriately. As you practice decreeing, declaring, and speaking life into yourself, God will use you to see and encourage new levels of expectancy in others. He will make you a blessing and encouragement to those around you.

CHAPTER 13

Prophecies

*I*n this chapter, I want to share some prophecies that have been delivered in our meetings. I am sharing them for a couple of reasons. First, so you can see some examples of how different individuals flow in the prophetic. Second, they are good words that could apply to your life now.

Each of these prophecies was delivered by a member of our ministry team. While some of them were for specific people who were present, others were for entire congregations.

God lives outside of time. Just because a word was delivered to other people at some point in the past does not mean it cannot apply to you in the present. As you read one of these prophetic words that agrees with your spirit, claim it for yourself, saying, "Yes, God, I receive that word for my life." Thank Him for it.

As you read these prophecies, examine them carefully and notice how they are worded and how they flow. They have undergone only minor editing to keep the integrity of the prophetic word intact. As you read each one, ask yourself, "Does it edify, encourage, exhort, provide direction, or serve as confirmation?" Look for those prophetic elements and learn from these examples. Enjoy!

PROPHETIC WORD FROM MELODY

During worship, I saw an image that looked like an electric fence that might be placed around a prison. God gave me the interpretation. There have been fences keeping you from your success. Those barriers are now weak, crumbling, and falling down. Your limitations are no longer there, so try again. God wants you to try again in those areas where you have experienced failure. He wants to bring you a new level of success in the future.

Although this was a word for that moment, all Christians can say, "God, I know You will elevate me to a new level of success. I trust You to help me break through to a new level where I have failed before."

Have you seen the movie *Jurassic Park*? Do you remember what the characters said about the animals testing the fences? They said the dinosaurs would never test the same area twice, but would always go to a different area. The animals remembered when the fence would not allow them to break through or when it hurt them.

God says, "I am removing and tearing down those barriers, those things that have kept you from moving into what I have called you to do. Try again." Test God yourself and you will know this is true.

PROPHETIC WORD FROM KELLEY

Prophetic ministries are usually very dynamic, with exhortation and powerful revelation. This particular meeting has been like a group hug because God wants you to know how much He loves you.

I had not planned to say anything, but just before the service started, the Lord gave me something for someone. For those of you who are not familiar with us, I do not want you to think that this is entirely revelatory. I know part of this because I have relationships with these people.

As the worship started, the Lord hit me with a message. I came into the service and sat down. God continued to talk to me for about twenty minutes. It seemed like I was not totally in one place or the other, but in between.

God wants to tell JB and Martha something. First, He wants you to know that He loves you. Martha volunteers at the ministry. We have known JB and Martha for years and love what they do for us and for God. Not too long ago, they had a family tragedy that changed their lives—their daughter died. I know that in the natural.

When I was sitting back there, God said to me, "In My house there are many dwelling places."

"That's good, Lord," I said, acknowledging that message from John 14:2. I related His words to JB and Martha: "God wants you to know that your daughter, Jackie, has one of those dwelling places."

Later, I had a vision. I do not have many visions. I have dreams, but this time I had a vision of Jackie leaning on a balustrade, looking down.

I had a mental picture of her throwing her parents kisses. She was pointing, clapping, and laughing. She was enthusiastic, which had been my observation when I met her.

Then I saw the Lord appear behind her. He put His hands on her, shook His head, and smiled. He was looking at JB and Martha too.

Hebrews 12:1 (NASB) says, "Therefore, since we have so great a cloud of witnesses ..." I just knew that vision meant that Jackie was watching her parents.

I told JB and Martha what I'd seen. Then I said, "God wants you to know that He is with her and she is with Him. She is keeping track of what is going on in your life. Although what happened to her was a tragedy, she is checking on you. That vision was God's way of saying, 'Your daughter is keeping in contact with you, and I am staying right here beside her.' He wants you to know that because He loves you so much."

Prophetic Words from Me

Kelley and I flow differently when it comes to the prophetic. He can get words weeks in advance and even writes them down. When I show up someplace, the Lord just drops a message into my spirit and that is what I release. I explain this because each person may receive and deliver a word in a different way.

I'm going to share some of the words I have delivered to people. Remember, if you hear a word and you want part of it, you can grab it for yourself. For instance, I once looked at a young couple and said, "The Lord is showing me millions coming your way. And He said, 'Keep your ears open, because there are new business ventures in your future.'" Do you want that for yourself? Then grab it!

When I saw a woman named Jessica, sitting next to her son, God gave me an image of him in college, studying on the Internet. I asked, *Lord, what is this about?*

I shared with Jessica's son the message I received for him. "God told me that you will be going to college, but you are also going to be studying online because the Lord is taking you around the world. I see you traveling with your parents, doing music in many countries. I also see you doing mission work."

I then told Jessica, "If you and Morgan do not have all your passports in place, get them ready. God said to start taking care of your personal business, get things in order, because you are going to be traveling very soon."

I also saw a woman who had longed for a mom her whole life. Every time someone became a mother figure to her, she was disappointed. I told her, "God says it is your time to step up and be a mom to other women who have no mother. Many other women have been crying out for someone to be their mothers, and He is sending them to you."

I once saw an older gentleman and I kept hearing, "The reverend. The reverend." I told him, "Sir, it is not by chance that you are here. I see you ministering not only in churches, but traveling and doing interviews on TV shows. I see you in magazines and writing books. I see books coming out quickly. Praise God!"

I once told a young woman, "There have been times when you felt like you were in the world and people could see you. At the same time, you felt all alone, invisible and insignificant. God says you do matter and He is going to use you. Although you are a big sister to many already, He is bringing you even more. I see young women coming to you who are cutters, on the verge of suicide. They know that if they sit down and talk to you, you will minister to them. You will hear from the Lord. They will not know that what you share is from the Lord, but they will know they are in a safe place. God says that you are His princess and He put you here for a purpose. You matter! Thank You, Jesus!"

I once told a couple named Steve and Sarah, "I see the Lord showing me a Spanish ministry in a completely new church. Because you have been loyal, He is going to start sending you to Latin nations. I hear Mexico calling you!"

I told them about a time when Pastor Marcus Davis was in Haiti, talking about the baptism of the Holy Spirit, and the fire of God fell like rain. All of a sudden, the floodwaters came down out of nowhere. "Steve," I said, "you are walking the same path, and I see you doing the same works with God. When you talk, I see the fire of God come out of you. God is showing me tongues of fire coming down as you release His word. I see miracles, signs, and wonders. I see you touching people and the dead being raised. Thank You, Jesus."

Another time, I told someone, "God wants you to stay in His peace and to not worry. You are not where you are by accident. He is clearing out a few things, but everything will soon fall into place."

After receiving a word for a newly published cookbook author, I told her, "Sugar, this is just your first book, because other books will come. Cooking is first, but I see your life as a script, not a book. I see a garment coming. Isn't that what they call clothes used in movies? I see your life before it became a script and how God transformed your life. I see women coming out of theaters with their chains left behind on the ground. Your story will set them free during that movie. Praise God!"

After a service where I had given several prophetic words, a young woman came up to me and said, "This isn't fair. What about me?"

I gave her the word God showed me in that moment. "You have been asking for clarity on which way to go. You have two options: working here or working where you will have the opportunity to travel to different locations. I see you taking that second job."

PROPHETIC WORD FROM MELODY WITH ACTIVATION PRAYER

When a man told me he was writing a book, I saw two books popping out of a toaster. After you put bread in a toaster, you press down the lever and the toasted bread pops up when it is ready. I told him, "There are going to be two books released at a time. They will come together rapidly and not need much time in the toaster. God is going to prepare you. At the right time, writing the books will be easy, without the difficulty of several drafts and proofs. The books will be completed and released easily."

Get into the Word so you will know what God is calling you to do. Seek His face. Pray, "God, thank You for releasing the gifts you have placed inside me."

At the end of an exciting evening service, I prayed, "Father, we thank You so much for tonight. Thank You for those words of encouragement. I thank You for pouring out healing. We thank You for being such a loving and gracious Father. Thank You for taking the time to speak to us. Thank You that You would use us to minister freedom, hope, and restoration to others. Father, we give You the glory for all You have done. I thank You for lives being changed and hearts being softened. Father, I thank You for bringing us to the right place at the right time to develop the release that is within us. Thank You for all the messages You will give us for those to whom we come in contact in the future. Amen."

CHAPTER 14

Prophetic Evangelism

Prophetic evangelism is witnessing and reaching out to unbelievers by hearing and delivering a specific word from God that addresses a person's need for salvation, healing, or deliverance. It is different from ordinary evangelism because it does not just preach the gospel. It speaks to an individual's life with a specific word from the Lord about his or her spiritual condition. It is not only a demonstration of the ability of the Word of God and the gospel of Jesus Christ to save, but also a display of God's power to minister specifically to each individual.

Everywhere I go, prophetic evangelism follows. This is not something we only do at church or ministry meetings, it is a way of life. And it is totally fun!

Our ministry team often eats at restaurants because we travel so much. If I am at a restaurant and see someone limping, I ask, "May I pray for you?" Most people are open to that. Frequently, one of us will get a prophetic word for a waiter or server, and we ask, "Would it be okay if I give you a word of encouragement?"

No one says no to that, because so few people give encouraging words to others.

People are blown away when God releases a specific word for them. It is incredible because all we are doing is listening to God and being obedient.

Many times, while I am talking to someone, I'll see a screen, and specific images pop up on it. I describe what I see to the person I'm talking to. Often people get different interpretations than I might have imagined.

As you go about your day, be sensitive to what God wants to say through you to other people. God orders your steps, and every person you see or encounter is in need of something. You migh have their answer. God may want to use you to deliver a word of encouragement to them. Be sensitive and ready to help others at all times.

PROPHETIC LIFE DIRECTION

God may speak in a prophetically symbolic way to give you direction. Several people who work for the ministry have received prophetic direction from God that led them to us. In the next pages, I will share a few of these examples.

Paulette Reed is a prophet. One day, she was walking around in Arizona and saw a Hunter-brand showerhead. She asked, "What are You telling me here, Lord?" A couple of months later, she moved to Texas to work with Joan Hunter Ministries. She was associated with our organization for some time. Now she travels the world and trains people to minister in the prophetic.

God can speak to you about the direction of your life through various things around you. If you pay attention and listen to what He says, you will recognize the ways He communicates.

Barbie Breathitt, who ministers at conferences at our ministry headquarters, told us that every so often she sees a dime on the floor. The Lord told her, "When you see a dime, be ready to turn on a dime." Now, each time she sees a dime, she knows something big is going to happen. God will use little things like that to reach you. When it happens, you will know He is speaking.

This ministry has a heart to serve people. Everywhere we go around the world, people are blessed with the love and compassion of our team members. Often, when we say good-bye, people do not want us to leave. They often ask, "Joan, do you really have to go?"

One young man fell in love with the Joan Hunter Ministries and was ordained through JHM in 2010. In 2011, he started traveling with our ministry team to various places as a volunteer. The first year was rough: he had to go to Hawaii and the Bahamas. Such a sacrifice. However, he also went to Haiti every few months, because that was where his heart was. He would serve with us for a month or so at a time, go back to New York to live with family for a month or two, then go back on the road.

One day, he was scheduled to go to New York to see his family, but he suddenly felt he was not supposed to be there. He asked God, "Lord, what's up with this?"

God said, "It's time for you to move. It's time for you to get rid of everything and be part of the ministry full time."

He sought counsel with his pastors. Then he shared what he thought with me, and I said, "It's about time. We've been waiting to hire you."

Although it was a sacrifice for him to not be around his family, he became a part of the JHM travel team for a time. When he got his first paycheck, he could not stop crying. He was amazed that he could get paid for doing something God had put in his heart.

Two years ago, God gave this man a vision. He was sitting with Jesus in lounge chairs looking over the heavens and the world, which was spinning. The Lord said, "Choose anywhere you want to go in the world and I will make a way."

The following week, he was with us for ordination. On the last day of ordination, Paulette Reed prophesied over each ordainee. When she finished, she gave this man a word. "I see the world spinning, and the Lord says, 'You choose anywhere you want to go and I will provide the way. Trust in Me.'"

The next day was New Year's Eve. I called to tell him, "The ministry just received a tremendous donation."

He responded, "Okay, I'm listening." I could tell he was excited because he thought I was calling to share a testimony with him.

"One of our partners works for a major airline. They have donated unlimited airfare to anywhere that airline flies around the world for a whole year. We have prayed over this blessing, and we want you to have it."

He immediately recalled that vision from two years ago. God had promised to provide no matter where he wanted to travel. His desire was to go all over the world. God blessed him with that ability.

EXAMPLES OF PROPHETIC EVANGELISM

One of the ways you can do prophetic evangelism is to conduct group treasure hunts. Break people up into groups of three or four and ask the Lord to show each of them different things. Have them follow the clues God gives to take them to the next place, or the next clue on your "prophetic treasure hunt."

One of our ministry team members shared the story of one

they did in New York. There were three people on his team, and they all had a vision of a woman. One saw her in a rainbow-colored shirt. Another saw fire in her hair. The third person heard the word *artist*. While they were walking in the Village, they saw a woman wearing a tie-dyed shirt, with fire-red hair, and she was an artist. When they approached her and told her their vision, she couldn't believe it. "Where did you people come from?" she asked. Then they were able to witness and minister to her.

Another time, a prophetic treasure hunt team saw a woman. One of the team members said, "I see numbers floating all around you. What kind of work do you do?"

She replied, "I am an accountant."

"The Lord sent us here," he said. "May we pray for you?"

"I really need prayer," she said. "I've been sitting here praying and I finally gave up." She accepted Jesus as her Lord and Savior that very day.

If you listen to the Holy Spirit, He can use you to minister to those around you in amazing ways. However, you have to be intentional about your prophetic ministry. Be sensitive to His voice and willing to take the risk. Whenever you have some extra time available, like if you're out running errands, take a minute and ask God to use you. Ask Him to lead you to someone you can pray with or encourage, someone you can bless that day.

As you go about your regular routine, listen to the still small voice of the Holy Spirit inside you and follow the promptings in your heart to speak to whoever God highlights. As you practice intentionally, this will become a habit and a regular occurrence in your life.

Here is another example of prophetic evangelism. One of our ministry team members was walking near a park when the Lord said, "Go into that park and talk to that woman."

He asked, *What woman?*

The Lord led him through the park to a woman sitting on a bench, crying. He approached her calmly and slowly, so as not to startle her, and said, "Ma'am?"

She looked up. "Yes?"

"The Lord sent me here to give you a word. He has heard your cries and He will keep His promise to take care of your family. Do not worry."

She started crying harder, so he backed up, hoping nobody would think he was making a woman in the park cry.

"I was so upset," she said, "I was crying out to the Lord. I left the house because my family is out of control. I said to God, 'If You're real, send me someone with a message that You will take care of my family. If You don't send me a message, I will not believe in You.'"

What if that team member was not willing to enter the park in search of a woman sitting on a bench? That woman may not have received the encouragement she desperately needed.

If you do not listen to God and obey His promptings, people's lives could be in danger. But if you are willing and obedient, God can use you to reach those around you. Take the time and do what He shows you to do. Miracles will happen!

After dinner at a friend's house, we all played a game. We formed a circle around a blindfolded person and walked around him until one of us got a word and said, "Stop!" Then that person released the word for the blindfolded person. The person who received the word put on the blindfold and we continued. Each time, the word delivered was correct.

There are many different ways to hear from God and practice your prophetic gifting. Find a group of trusted friends, practice flowing in the prophetic, and watch what God will do.

There may be times when you receive a word but you don't want to share it. For instance, many of the JHM ministry staff members attend Pastor Marcus Davis's church, and they are always hungry to get a word from God. One day, an employee received a word that he did not want to share. Everyone else was giving words about things they were going through and how the Lord had touched them and changed their lives. He told the Lord, *I don't want to stop that flow. If You want this word to be released, You will have to tell Marcus.*

As Marcus started the service, he walked down the aisle and said, "The Lord said my friend has a word." He handed this man the microphone.

Things like this will happen when you are obedient and listen to God. You will release prophetic words whenever, wherever, and however God wants you to.

There are many ways to hear God's voice, but do not take the process for granted. God will keep His promises and He will fulfill His word to you.

CHAPTER 15

Activation Exercise

To empower the people who were attending one of my conferences, we performed a prophetic activation exercise. I asked everyone in the room to close their eyes. I asked everyone who was watching the conference over the Internet to do the same. Then I went through the group and touched one person who would be the recipient of the prophetic words. No one else knew which person I had touched, so they really had to step out on faith that the word they were receiving was from God.

When I felt that all of the words had been delivered, I prayed a simple activation prayer. "Father, I ask You to give words of encouragement, edification, and confirmation regarding this person who has been touched this evening. Father, I thank You for giving words that will completely transform this person. In Jesus' name, amen."

After everyone opened their eyes, I asked the individuals who had received words to come forward.

One man walked up to the front and shared the following. "I saw a veil in front of you. It was not completely solid, but it impaired your vision somewhat so you could not clearly see what was in front of you. After Jesus prayed for the blind man, He asked, "What do you see?" And the blind man said, "I see men as trees, walking."[3] It has been like that spiritually for you because you have desired to take hold of and grasp what God has for you. You hear great testimonies of wonderful miracles, but you may feel as if you are only experiencing a minimum of what you know God wants you to have. You are seeing through a veil.

"God is pulling back the veil and making things clear for you. He is pulling away the hindrances that have clouded your vision so that you can experience the miracles and breakthroughs He has for you in a much greater way. Be encouraged! The blessing you seek is right in front of you, even though it has seemed very far away because of this veil. God is removing the generational hindrances and condemnation you have been feeling and the things that have been hindering your faith in those areas where you know you are supposed to be progressing. God is taking all of that away so that you can step into and experience the fullness of His miraculous love and power."

"Hallelujah," I responded. "That is a good word for all of us."

After that, people seemed hesitant to come forward. I said, "Some of you may have just a simple word like *beautiful* or *handsome* or *daybreak*. Come up and share. Don't feel, *Oh, that word was eloquent. I cannot do that.* Don't worry. This is a training session, meant to activate you to step out into a new realm.

A woman came forward and said, "I have one phrase. 'You

---

3 See Mark 8:24 KJV.

have a spirit of excellence about you.' I also heard one word: *college*. I don't know what it means."

I told the group, "There are many ways in which that could be interpreted. We offer college here at JHM, without accreditation. It could mean that someone is to go back to college, or their children or grandchildren will go to college. It could also mean a college debt will be paid off."

Another woman said, "When I had my eyes closed, I got a picture of a wishbone. God's hand was pulling one side, and the other side was being pulled by a person's hand. I asked, *What does this mean, Lord?* And He said, *No matter what, whichever side, you still have My favor.*"

"That is awesome," I said. "When you see a wishbone, that means favor. When you say the word *favor,* you might get another word or be able to finish the thought."

Another woman said, "The only word I have is *tomorrow.* It's only one word, but I believe it is significant."

"That word means the prophecy is not for now, but for *tomorrow.* When is tomorrow? It could be the following day or next week or later."

One man said, "I heard the word *cultivate* about two weeks ago. And I heard it again today."

"That could refer to a double portion," I said. "This is very exciting. When you find out who the person is, and when she explains what these words mean to her, you will understand the messages you were given for her."

One woman said, "I saw a waterfall."

"That represents the Holy Spirit's ministry."

Another woman said, "I saw a beautiful little horse with a beautiful blonde mane. It is waiting for your love. You own it already." After a short pause, she said, "I wasn't going to say anything, but the Lord kept telling me, *It's important.*"

"You are supposed to sit, listen, ask, and obey," I said. "God will speak to you if you just ask."

When no one else spoke up, I asked Kelly, the woman I'd touched, to come up. I had known Kelly for a few weeks, so I was aware of a few things about her. But she didn't seem to be close friends with anyone else in the room.

I asked Kelly to share what God had put on her heart through those prophetic words.

"Kelly, do you own horses?" I asked.

"Yes," she said. "My childhood dream was to train horses. I have three of them. And one has a blonde mane."

"That is so cool!" I said.

Kelly continued. "My grandson has been asking lately, 'Can we read the Word when we get up in the morning?' Usually, in the mornings, we get busy right away and we don't take time to read the Bible. That is going to change. That veil has been keeping us from His truth."

I shivered with excitement. "And what does *college* mean to you?"

Kelly shrugged. "College would be sitting here and learning about the prophetic."

I couldn't stop grinning. "And *cultivate*?"

Kelly took a deep breath. "My family owns a farm, so we cultivate—sowing, growing, and reaping. My prayer is that everything I do is in excellence to Him."

"Because you have been sowing and cultivating spiritually, God is going to give you a double portion on your land. It will multiply, but you will also have a greater multiplication in your finances."

Kelly smiled. "Our property is up for sale."

I put my hand on her shoulder. "We will trust God that you will get twice as much as you're asking for it."

I then checked our online responses and found that three words had come in for Kelly from people who were watching on the Internet.

"Someone heard the word *butter,* I told the group. We can interpret *butter* in several different ways. Kelly loves to cook and does it for many people. Butter is also rich oil. It is stronger than virgin olive oil and blends well. So it can symbolize a rich anointing."

One person from the Internet wrote, "I see a royal crown of solid gold with lots and lots of flowers."

"If I got a crown," I said, "I would prefer one with jewels. But Kelly's favorite thing is flowers, so God honoring her with a crown filled with flowers is perfect for her."

The third word an Internet follower shared was *orange blossom*—also a flower. I am from Florida, and the state flower is the orange blossom, which has a wonderful fragrance. "If you smell the fragrance of God," I said, "ninety-nine percent of the time it will smell like orange blossoms. Kelly loves the presence of the Lord, the fragrance of the Lord, so that is a significant revelation for her. Hallelujah!"

This was a special way to practice listening to God. The Lord gave us some wonderful words. I especially love that picture of a long, flowing, blonde mane because Kelly is blonde and she loves horses.

MORE EXAMPLES OF PROPHETIC WORDS

When the prophetic is in operation, God can give download after download of encouraging words for people.

The following words were delivered during a conference where our team was training people on prophetic ministry. It is usually best to learn by demonstration and example. I call this "pray-teach." I pray for people and teach them how to pray at the same time.

Based on what you've read in this book, see if you can identify the different characteristics of prophetic ministry in these examples.

And remember, if something you read here applies to you and your life, claim it for yourself. Even though these words were given at a specific location, at a specific time, and to specific people, they are not limited to those people or that time. If any message here is for you, receive it and thank God for His blessing.

Prophetic Word #1

A long time before that conference, God gave me a word for somebody who worked at the Joan Hunter Ministries. I had wanted to speak this word over him ever since, but God did not release me to speak until that day.

When God gives you a word, you may have to wait patiently until He releases you to speak it. You cannot blurt out everything that pops into your head. Prophetic ministry doesn't work that way. Even if you love someone and want to bless him or her, releasing the word has to be directed by God, not by your personal idea or desire.

When God finally released me to deliver this word to my friend and colleague, here is what God told him through me: "This is a year of blessing for you and a year of refreshing. You have been wounded, full of emptiness, loneliness, and disappointment. This will be a year for God to take those things away and restore your soul. This is a year of restoration and renewal."

God did not tell me what that meant. I imagined maybe he'd get a new car or a new house. But God said, "Tell him one of these blessings will be wearing a smile." A car or house doesn't smile, does it?

I then said to this man, "I saw God peeling off your old skin and making you new. The painful stuff from your past is being removed. I see new beginnings, a transformation, and a completely new life for you. God knows your heart's desire, and I see you in a new community. You are not leaving here, but He has a new life for you. It is time for change. The spirit of joy is coming upon you."

This was a powerful word for the person who received it because he, as well as several others who were present when it was delivered, had lost a great deal.

Perhaps that's true for you too. But rejoice! This is a year of godly restoration. He is going to take the loneliness from many hearts.

Prophetic Word #2

I then heard a word for someone who might have been watching the conference via the Internet. "A woman named Stephanie is stressed out right now. There is a lot of tension in your body and you probably need a massage. God says, 'Stephanie, relax.' He is in control, so you don't need to be. He will resolve your situation in His own way."

Prophetic Word #3

One of my colleagues got a word for someone at the conference named Debra. "You are on the verge of a new beginning," he said.

"I see a moving truck coming to your house and I hear the word *downsizing*. God is downsizing your living space to give you the freedom to fulfill your heart's desire. God is giving you free passage around the world to do what you are called to do and what you have been crying out to do. God said you do not have to cry anymore.

This man did not know that I'd had conversations with Debra and she'd been in my prayers.

When I asked Debra to confirm this word, she shared with the audience that she had indeed been planning to move. She had put her house on the market. She wanted to travel with the ministry. The word my colleague delivered served as additional confirmation for Debra that God was behind this move.

That is the way prophetic ministry should function. Confirmation is a key component of prophecy.

Prophetic Word #4

Shortly before that conference, God brought a famous poem to my mind: "Footprints in the Sand," written by Mary Stevenson in 1936. The poem speaks of two sets of footprints on the sand heading down a path—a person's and Jesus'. When the person reaches the end of the journey and looks back, only one set of footsteps remains. At first the person questions the reason for having to walk the journey alone. But Jesus explains that He carried the person through life.

At the conference, I said, "Somebody here has that 'Footprints in the Sand' poem hanging on the wall of your house. God wants you to know that He is picking you up and carrying you. He wants to tell you His steps are in front of you and you are moving forward. His steps are leaving footprints because He is heavy. One of the aspects of His glory is that it has great weight.

You are stepping into His heavy footsteps. Obedience is the essential action for you to walk in His footsteps."

Prophetic Word #5

I also received a word for a brother who was watching the conference online. "The Lord says He has heard you calling out. You have made sacrifices and you've been in wrong relationships over the years because you did things your way. You have surrendered to Him, but whenever you are at a point of frustration, you need to step back, repent, and say, 'Lord, I still trust You. I know You are going to bring the right woman to me.' God said this woman is coming, and by this summer, you will know her."

Prophetic Word #6

I received this word for a person named Rachel. I heard God say, "Rachel, do not fight it. This is from Me, and I will make this as palatable as possible. Change is necessary to do what I want you to do. My heart is full of love for you and I will make a way where there is no way. Rachel, trust Me!"

Prophetic Word #7

This word was for a man wearing a red sweater. "The Lord is saying that He has not forgotten you. He wants you to know that you are His favorite and He loves you. Do not ever forget that."

Prophetic Word #8

To somebody named John, I gave this word. "Above all, God wants you to know that He loves you. God specifically wants you to read John 3:30, where John the Baptist is talking about Jesus. John said, 'He must increase and I must decrease.' God wants you to know that, John."

Prophetic Word #9

After a detailed vision, I proclaimed, "I see a book table that is stretching out before me, covered with many books written by someone in this room. Many people are downloading your books from the Internet. People will be asking you for the rights to translate your books into many languages. It is time."

This word was for someone who was present at the conference. But that night, I had a conversation with someone who told me he'd heard about the word I gave earlier that day. He told me, "About ten years ago, I received a prophetic word saying, "Books, books, books. There are books inside of you. Get those books out. Write those books!" He had been writing ever since. He had written five books in the last five years.

The Lord showed him that the apostle Paul was a face-to-face, one-on-one type of person. Paul was an avid traveler. He continuously moved from one place to another to minister to people. His passion was to spread the word about Jesus to the whole earth. When he went into a city, he started a church, helped people train leaders, and then moved on to the next city. He did this over and over.

When he ended up in prison, Paul's normal contact with people was severely limited. His only interaction with others was through writing letters. This seemingly insignificant work elevated him to an entirely new level. His letters became part of God's precious Word, the Bible. His influence has reached nations worldwide throughout the generations. Today we still read, believe, and stand on those letters written during Paul's lonely days in prison.

Would Paul have written those letters if he had not been stuck in prison so many times? The Lord used his circumstances as a quiet time to write most of the New Testament.

That prophecy confirmed to this man I spoke with after my conference that writing the books that God had placed in his heart was very important.

Last summer, Joan Hunter Ministries produced, printed, and released his latest book. His writings will be translated into many languages and go around the world, as was prophesied.

Prophetic Word #10

I received a word at that conference about cars. In spiritual language, a car represents your ministry. It can also be a way by which God is getting you to where He wants you to be so you can do what He wants you to do.

"Miracles will happen this year," I proclaimed. "Many people are struggling to find their place and have been unfulfilled because they are doing other things. This year is the time for you to find your car. When you do, get in and fasten your seatbelt. If that is true for you and you receive this word, you will not be able to stay where you are and continue doing what you are presently doing.

"You will be moving, not staying in the same position. The past cannot be the guide for your future. It got you here, but from now on, you have a new set of rules to follow. You are going to a new place by a new path and you will do things differently. The things you used to rely on will not work very well, if they work at all.

"Work hard. What God does in this next season will be greatly accelerated. His work has been slowly building the last few years. The time between planting (seedtime) and harvest is getting shorter because God is speeding up that process. In fact, Amos 9:13 says there will be a time when the one who plows will overtake the one who sows. That cannot happen in the natural realm, only in the supernatural realm.

"Relocations are imminent for many. Some of you are going to move, and the transplant process is unavoidable. Many will be surrounded by new subcultures: languages, ethnicities, economies, lifestyles, and thought processes. Many will ask, 'What am I doing here? These people are not like me.'

"God says that those whom you say are not your people are, indeed, your people. Those areas you say are not your region are, indeed, where God wants you to be. Get ready for some necessary mental and emotional adjustments."

Prophetic Word #11

When my husband, Kelley, was flowing in the prophetic, he used the word *supernatural*. Sensing a word from the Lord for someone specific, I added, "When you heard the word *supernatural* just now, your heart lit up like *ding, ding, ding, ding*. I believe that everywhere you go—hanging out with your friends, home groups, or church—you can expect supernatural things to happen. I see jewels and gold dust falling, and oil coming from your hands and your feet. I see things that have never been done before. This year is an open door. You will be stepping through new doors and have many new experiences."

Prophetic Word #12

The Lord gave me an example of repositioning people, which I shared with the attendees at the conference. "In the eighteen hundreds, there was a reorganization of nation states by colonial powers. The Europeans forced people groups along certain lines to become nations, which did not make a lot of sense. In the nineteen hundreds, most of those nations failed and dissolved. Yugoslavia became five countries, the Soviet Union broke up into many pieces, and African nations became two or three nations along tribal lines.

"In this century, there will be another reorganization of nation states along a new set of lines. God is going to put some of you in a place to influence the social and economic changes in the new nation states that will be birthed."

Prophetic Word #13

To a man in a checkered shirt, I said, "I see you working with men. You are probably asking, 'Why me?' God will lead men to you for ministry. God said you have a father's heart to help others, and because your heart is so large, He will use you. Many lost souls need a father, and He will bring them to you."

Prophetic Word #14

I also delivered this word to the conference attendees. "This is a time of increasing government intrusion worldwide in every area of our lives. People used to say, 'Government cannot legislate morality.' I believe the liberal-leaning governments of the current era are doing exactly that, legislating morality. Fortunately, the Scripture has a few things to say about an era where evil is called good and good is called evil, and darkness is substituted for light and bitterness is substituted for sweet.

"Isaiah 59:19 says, 'From the west, people will fear the name of the Lord, and from the rising of the sun, they will revere his glory. For he will come like a pent-up flood that the breath of the Lord drives along.'

"There was a span of four hundred years between the last prophecy of the Old Testament and the coming of Jesus. However, there was one man who called the people to repentance before Jesus came on the scene. His name was John the Baptist. His message was to prepare the way for the Messiah. He indeed called people to repentance and then baptized many.

"God will use us to do the same. By the Holy Spirit, He will raise us up as a standard to call people to repentance. Merely railing against the sins of our culture—abortion, homosexuality, drug abuse, infidelity, etc.—is not going to change anything. In fact, people proudly congratulate themselves on their sins and seek others to celebrate their addictions.

"Philippians 3:19 says, 'Their destiny is destruction, their god is their stomach, and their glory is in their shame. Their mind is set on earthly things.' Is there any better verse to characterize our current culture?

"I want to make it very clear that you are that voice crying from the wilderness in today's world. You are the John the Baptist of today. Your words will make crooked ways straight, preparing the way of the Lord, the return of our King."

Prophetic Word #15

I delivered a word that I believed many would want to grab. "Madam, you are looking at your computer and screaming, 'I have given scripturally. I have done everything the right way as I know it. Why have my finances not changed?' The Lord says, 'Enough is enough. I am tearing down those hindrances today.'"

PRAYER OF ACTIVATION

In this book, I do not want to only give you information and knowledge about prophecy. I want to demonstrate the prophetic to you, show you how it works, and allow you to see how easy it can be. Anyone who desires to prophesy can do it ... including *you!*

Here are some steps to activate the prophetic word in you:

1. Honor the prophet.

2. Believe God will give you the word and will fulfill what He says.

3. Watch your mouth so you don't cancel your blessings.

4. Pray, confirm, and discern God's voice.

5. Walk in obedience to His voice.

You do not have to be a full-time pastor or in a Charismatic ministry to be a vessel for God to flow through you prophetically. Any believer can do it. Now that you are equipped with this knowledge and all of these examples, you can do it too!

I want to encourage you to pray this prayer of activation with me aloud.

Father, I thank You for the material that You have provided through this book as well as other studies and experiences I have had in prophetic ministry. I ask You to take this knowledge and activate it in my life. In Jesus' name, I pray that You would open my ears, my eyes, and my heart to receive the messages You send me. I pray that You would give me the courage and boldness required to take the step of faith needed in order to deliver Your messages to those waiting to receive. I ask You to direct my steps and to lead me to the people who need to receive ministry from You and that you would open their hearts to receive Your words. I am willing. I am available. I am ready to speak Your word to others. Use me for Your glory. In Jesus' name. Amen."

Now take the step of faith. Get out there and practice sharing the prophetic words God has given you. Are you ready? Let's go!

JoanHunter.org